BrightRED Study Guide

Curriculum for Excellence

N5

ADMINISTRATION
and IT

Claire Cooper and Raymond Simpson

BrightRED
PUBLISHING

First published in 2014 by:
Bright Red Publishing Ltd
1 Torphichen Street
Edinburgh
EH3 8HX

MIX
Paper from
responsible sources
FSC® C013254

A CIP record for this book is available from the British Library

ISBN 978-1-906736-31-6

With thanks to:
PDQ Digital Media Solutions Ltd (layout) and Sue Moody, Bright Writing (edit)

Cover design and series book design by Caleb Rutherford – e i d e t i c

Acknowledgements
Every effort has been made to seek all copyright holders. If any have been overlooked, then Bright Red Publishing will be delighted to make the necessary arrangements.

Permission has been sought from all relevant copyright holders and Bright Red Publishing are grateful for the use of the following:
shironosov/iStock.com (page 7); stockyimages/iStock.com (page 8); Minerva Studio/iStock.com (page 9); Signs © Health & Safety Executive. Contains public sector information published by the Health and Safety Executive and licensed under the Open Government Licence (pages 10, 13 & 17); ginosphotos/iStock.com (page 11); banj0e/iStock.com (page 12); innovatedcaptures/iStock.com (page 12); Lydia (CC BY 2.0)[1] (page 14); mariakraynova/iStock.com (page 14); eyjafjallajokull/iStock.com (page 14); gemphoto/Shutterstock.com (page 15); Chad McDermott/Shutterstock.com (page 17); monkeybusinessimages/iStock.com (page 18); Jimmy and Sasha (CC BY-ND 2.0)[2] Reade (page 23); Darumo/iStock.com (page 24); Keri J (CC BY-ND 2.0)[2] (page 25); maximili/iStock.com (page 25); wyrls/freeimages.com (page 25); ScotRail (page 26); vladacanon/iStock.com (page 27); Ever/iStock.com (page 27); pay404/iStock.com (page 60); monkeybusinessimages/iStock.com (page 66); fazon1/iStock.com (page 70); ASDA (page 70); Logos for Outlook & Hotmail used with permission from Microsoft®. Logo for LYCOS® is a registered trademark of Lycos, Inc. in the United States and other countries (page 86); rafal_olechowski/iStock.com (page 88); pressureUA/iStock.com (page 88).

Permission to reproduce extracts from [BS 5261-2:2005] is granted by BSI. British Standards can be obtained in PDF or hard copy formats from the BSI online shop: www.bsigroup.com/Shop or by contacting BSI Customer Services for hardcopies only: Tel: +44 (0)20 8996 9001, Email: cservices@bsigroup.com (page 55).

(CC BY 2.0)[1] http://creativecommons.org/licenses/by/2.0/
(CC BY-ND 2.0)[2] http://creativecommons.org/licenses/by-nd/2.0/

Printed and bound in the UK.

CONTENTS

THE NATIONAL 5 COURSE

COURSE CONTENT AND ASSESSMENT

THE UNITS

The Administration and IT course consists of three units:
- Administrative Practices
- IT Solutions for Administrators
- Communication in Administration

All three units are mandatory and provide the content on which you will be assessed in both the unit assessments and the course assignment. Here is an outline of each unit.

ADMINISTRATIVE PRACTICES

This Unit provides a broad introduction to the administrative function within the workplace, and will enable you to complete a series of administrative tasks within the context of organising and supporting events. On completion of this Outcome, you will have developed an understanding of:
- the tasks, skills and qualities of an administrator
- customer care
- Health and Safety in the workplace
- security of people, property and information.

IT SOLUTIONS FOR ADMINISTRATORS

This unit aims to develop your skills in using IT. It also aims to develop your ability to problem-solve, organise and manage information within the context of administrative-related scenarios. You will select appropriate IT software applications, including word processing, spreadsheets and databases and use them to create and edit business documents. On completion of this Outcome, you will have developed practical abilities in the use of:
- Spreadsheets
  - formatting
  - functions
  - charting
  - printing
- Databases
  - inputting and editing data
  - sorting and searching
  - forms and reports
  - printing
- Word processing
  - editing business documents
  - creating and editing tables
  - integrating information from another software package
  - mail merging
  - printing

COMMUNICATION IN ADMINISTRATION

This unit aims to develop the skills you need to gather and share information in administrative-based scenarios. On completion of this Outcome, you will have developed skills in and/or knowledge of:
- searching for and extracting relevant information from various sources
- the features of reliable sources of information
- the consequences of using unreliable internet sources of information
- using advanced functions of technology to prepare and communicate information
- creating and amending presentations
- using desktop publishing to produce documents
- using e-mail, blogs, podcasts, websites, social media and other emerging technologies
- using e-diaries.

ASSESSMENT

For the course assessment, you need to pass three Unit Assessments during the course of the year and complete a final course assignment. The course assignment is a practical assessment. It is designed to assess your ability to apply the Administration and IT skills you have developed over the year, within the context of organising and supporting an event. The assignment will have 100 marks.

You must complete the entire closed book assignment under supervised conditions over a period not exceeding four hours. You will have to complete the assignment independently of the teacher/lecturer. The assignment will be externally assessed. The assignment has two stages:

contd

STAGE 1

Stage 1 involves completing tasks relevant to an event and could include:

- preparing a to-do/priorities list
- entering details into an e-diary
- searching for information about the venue and resources and how to book them
- using spreadsheets to access relevant statistical or financial information, including the budget for the event
- using appropriate software to prepare the agenda
- using appropriate software to prepare materials such as name badges, advertising, invitations and place-cards
- using databases to store details of delegates/performers and to carry out the following functions: update, search, mail-merge and prepare letters, labels, attendees' report
- using presentation software to prepare the key speaker's presentation, background/welcoming presentation
- resolve a double-booking of the venue
- prepare additional documents at short notice
- changing travel or other arrangements due to unforeseen circumstances.

STAGE 2

Stage 2 involves completing follow-up tasks that could include:

- preparing an evaluation of the event
- collating responses and present findings in a variety of formats, including charts
- preparing 'thank you' letters (to the venue host, participants and guests), using mail-merge
- preparing minutes, notes or action points
- preparing event costings and expenses.

Marks will be awarded for demonstrating skills in the use of the different IT applications, and for knowledge and understanding of administration in the workplace.

Exam content	Mark allocation
Spreadsheets Databases Word processing Desktop publishing Communication	Each of these IT applications will feature in the assignment and the allocation of marks will be: 18 marks(+/- 3 marks)
Knowledge and Understanding	15 marks (+/- 5 marks)
Total	100 marks

GRADES

You will be given a final grade (A–D) based on your performance in the assignment. A brief description of the standard required to achieve each grade is given below:

Grade A   You will have to demonstrate a high level of performance in relation to the mandatory skills, knowledge and understanding for the course. You will normally have to achieve above 70 per cent in the final assignment to be awarded a Grade A.

Grade B   You will have to demonstrate a strong level of performance in relation to the mandatory skills, knowledge and understanding for the course. You will normally have to achieve 60–69 per cent in the final assignment to be awarded a Grade B.

Grade C   You will have to demonstrate a good level of performance in relation to the mandatory skills, knowledge and understanding for the course. You will normally have to achieve 50–59 per cent in the final assignment to be awarded a Grade C.

Grade D   You will have to demonstrate an adequate level of performance in relation to the mandatory skills, knowledge and understanding for the course. You will normally have to achieve 45–49 per cent in the final assignment to be awarded a Grade D.

For all awards – you need to have achieved all of the National Unit assessments for the course, in addition to passing the final assignment.

 ONLINE

This book is supported by the Bright Red Digital Zone – head to www.brightredbooks.net/N5AdminIT for extra links, videos, tests and more.

PROVIDING AN ACCOUNT OF ADMINISTRATION IN THE WORKPLACE

TASKS, SKILLS AND QUALITIES OF ADMINISTRATORS

OUTCOME 1: AN OVERVIEW

For Outcome 1 of this unit, you are required to:

1 Provide an account of administration in the workplace by:

    1.1 Describing tasks, skills and qualities of an administrative assistant

    1.2 Describing the key features of good customer care in the context of administration

    1.3 Describing the organisational responsibilities in terms of health and safety

    1.4 Describing the key organisational responsibilities in terms of security of people, property and information.

WHAT TASKS DO ADMINISTRATORS CARRY OUT IN THE WORKPLACE?

Look at this job advert for an Administrative Assistant for an idea of the tasks carried out by administrators in the workplace:

Administrative Assistant

Full-time with flexi-time option available. Permanent contract available once six-month probation period completed.

£15 500 rising to £16 250 after completion of probation. We are currently recruiting for an Administrative Assistant to work in our Marketing Department.

The post will require the successful candidate to deal with:

- Reception duties
- Mail handling
- Reprographics
- Answering the telephone and responding to e-mails
- Petty cash

We are looking for candidates who possess excellent communication skills and who can confidently use integrated IT packages – in particular Microsoft Word, Access and Excel. Candidates are not required to have previous experience, although this would be an advantage. For more information about the role, please refer to the Person Specification on our website. To apply, please visit our website by clicking the *apply now* link.

DESCRIBING TASKS, SKILLS AND QUALITIES OF AN ADMINISTRATIVE ASSISTANT

Tasks and skills are the roles, responsibilities or duties of an Administrative Assistant. They are the day-to-day activities that the Administrative Assistant is responsible for. These might be:

Tasks/duties	Skills/qualities required
Answering the telephone or responding to e-mails/written correspondence	• excellent communication skills • professional attitude • a good knowledge of business practices
Mail handling	• interpersonal skills • organisational skills • pays attention to detail
Preparing business documents: • business letters • reports • agendas and minutes of meetings	• excellent IT skills – ability to use various packages • pays attention to detail • ability to work independently or as part of a team
Reception duties: • dealing with visitors to the organisation • managing diaries and the appointments book	• excellent communication skills • interpersonal skills • organisational skills • ability to manage time • problem-solving skills • professional attitude
Sourcing information: • using the internet to locate information • making travel arrangements • making preparations for meetings and events	• excellent IT skills • excellent communication skills • organisational skills

WHAT IS THE DIFFERENCE BETWEEN A SKILL AND A QUALITY?

A **skill** is an ability that is gained through learning and training, whereas a **quality** is a personal characteristic – an aspect of your personality.

Skills	Qualities
communication skills interpersonal skills organisational skills problem-solving skills IT skills	ability to manage time professional attitude approachable manner pays attention to detail

A **Job Description** for an Administrative Assistant will outline the background to the role, the tasks/duties to be carried out, the employee's responsibilities and who they report to. It might also include their days/hours of work, pay grade and benefits.

A **Person Specification** details the skills, qualities, qualifications and experience that a suitable candidate is required to have.

ONLINE

Head to www. brightredbooks.net/ N5AdminIT and have a look at the examples of a Job Description and a Person Specification.

ONLINE TEST

Test yourself on 'Tasks, Skills and Qualities of Administrators' at www. brightredbooks.net/ N5AdminIT

THINGS TO DO AND THINK ABOUT

Use the S1 jobs website to search for an Administrator job in your area. Compare the Job Description and Person Specification with the ones above.

CUSTOMER CARE

Customer service is the process of ensuring that the customer feels that the product or service they have bought has met or exceeded their expectations.

DESCRIBING THE KEY FEATURES OF GOOD CUSTOMER CARE

Most organisations need customers to survive. It's for that reason that most organisations invest heavily in training their employees to provide excellent customer service at all times.

Customer care is about:

- treating your customers with respect at all times
- communicating well with customers before, during and after the sale/service
- getting it right first time – if a customer is unhappy, the organisation needs to sort out the issue as quickly as possible.

BENEFITS OF GOOD CUSTOMER SERVICE

The benefits of good customer service are:

- attracting new customers and retaining existing customers
- building customer loyalty
- developing a good reputation
- increased Market Share
- increased sales/profits

CUSTOMER SERVICE STRATEGIES

Some key strategies used by organisations to ensure good customer service are:

- Customer service policy – a document detailing how the customer will be treated by the organisation.
- Customer loyalty scheme – a reward scheme for customers who use the organisation regularly.
- Complaints procedure – a detailed description of the way in which complaints are handled by the organisation.
- Customer service training for all staff – comprehensive training for all staff to ensure that they are providing consistent service to all customers at all times.
- Ongoing evaluation of customer satisfaction – through mystery shoppers, comments cards and customer surveys.
- Measuring the quality of the customer experience to ensure consistency – this feedback will also help the business to improve in the future.

contd

DON'T FORGET

Market Share is the percentage of total sales from one industry which belong to one company. For example, a supermarket chain may hold 30% Market Share of groceries in the UK.

The following is the Customer Care Charter for Angus Council.
Angus Council will:
- treat you politely and with respect
- be friendly and approachable
- listen to what you have to say
- respect your right to confidentiality
- be open and accountable
- give you the information you need about our services
- give you choice in how you access services
- value and respect the diversity of our customers and try to meet the needs of customers with specific requirements
- work in partnership with other organisations and communities to improve our services
- learn from your compliments, comments and complaints.

CONSEQUENCES OF POOR CUSTOMER SERVICE

An organisation's failure to recognise the importance of its customers can have serious consequences. These might include:

- a poor reputation as a result of customers sharing their experiences with friends and family

- a fall in customer numbers

- bad publicity, leading to a fall in sales and then profits

- demotivated staff, leading to an increase in staff turnover

- eventual business closure

DON'T FORGET

Successful customer care is when you retain your customers because they have been more than satisfied with your goods or services.

ONLINE TEST

Test yourself on 'Customer care' at www.brightredbooks.net/N5AdminIT.

VIDEO LINK

Check out the clip about how to provide customer care at www.brightredbooks.net/N5AdminIT

VIDEO LINK

Have a look at some examples of bad customer service at www.brightredbooks.net/N5AdminIT

THINGS TO DO AND THINK ABOUT

Identify a local company and find out what their customer care policies are.

HEALTH AND SAFETY

Businesses are legally bound by the Health and Safety at Work Act (HASWA) 1974. This legislation is in place to ensure that employers provide a safe working environment for their employees to work in.

DESCRIBING THE ORGANISATIONAL RESPONSIBILITIES IN TERMS OF HEALTH AND SAFETY

The HASWA details the responsibilities of both the employer and the employee:

Employers' responsibilities	Employees' responsibilities
Ensure that the Health and Safety Policy is clearly displayed and that all employees are aware of its content.	Carry out their duties in a safe manner, without putting their colleagues at risk.
Perform regular risk assessments to ensure a safe working environment.	Ensure that they carry out their responsibilities as assigned to them through the Health and Safety Policy.
Provide employees with training opportunities to ensure that they are aware of all Health and Safety responsibilities.	Report any faults, damage or spillages that could cause harm to themselves or others.
Provide protective clothing and equipment when required.	Use the protective clothing or equipment if issued to them for use in the workplace.

INDUCTION TRAINING

New recruits to a company need basic induction training so that they know how to work safely. This includes finding out about arrangements for first aid, fire and evacuation.

EXAMPLE:

Here is a list of the important topics in Dawlish Town Council's induction training:

Fire safety
- What to do if the fire alarm goes off.
- How to get out of the building (including alternative exits) and where to assemble.
- What to do if the staff member discovers a fire.
- Location of fire action notices, alarm call points, fire extinguishers.
- Importance of not using fire extinguishers unless trained to do so.

First-aid and accident reporting
- How to get first-aid in the event of an accident.
- The importance of reporting accidents and how to report them.
- Names of the first-aiders in the building where the staff member is based.
- Location of first-aid equipment and room.

Organisation for health and safety
- Line managers' responsibility for health and safety.
- The role of the Health Safety and Welfare Officer.
- Specialist occupational health advice and how to get it.

- The role of the maintenance staff in ensuring safety.
- How to report items needing maintenance.
- Extent of individual responsibility for health and safety.

Communication and consultation
- The existence of the Council Health and Safety Policy. Opportunity should be given for the new staff member to inspect the corporate policy and any departmental policies.
- The existence of the Health Safety and Welfare Forum.
- Union Health and Safety representatives.
- Health and Safety notice boards and the poster 'Health and Safety Law: what you should know'.

Council rules
- The no-smoking policy and its importance in fire prevention.
- Any local rules or procedures that the new member of staff will be expected to follow.

HAZARDS IN THE WORKPLACE

Hazard	Safe practice
Blocking fire exits.	Keep all fire exits closed and freely accessible.
Wires and cables becoming trip hazards.	Use cable protectors and extension cables to ensure there are no tripping hazards
Poor lighting causing eye-strain and headaches.	Ensure there are enough lights and of the right brightness. Replace any flickering bulbs.
Light glare from outside causing eye-strain and headaches.	Fit computer screens with glare guards or have blinds on all windows.
Work stations being at inappropriate heights, causing back strain.	Ensure all workstations are adjusted to the staff working at them.
Liquid spills, causing staff to fall.	A wet floor sign should be put in place until spill has been cleared up.
Electrical equipment not regularly checked or inappropriately used can cause electrical shocks.	Ensure yearly checks on electrical equipment and do not allow un-trained staff to use.
Unstable filing cabinets, which could fall onto staff.	Ensure cabinets are stable, fixed to walls and have appropriate weight in the bottom.
Excessive heat or cold.	Ensure that a ventilation system is in place to keep temperatures to acceptable norms.
Inappropriate seats, resulting in back strain.	Ensure that all seats are variable in height and ensure your staff sit correctly.
Excessive noise, causing headaches and illness.	Move noisy equipment to another room or use noise shields.

ACCIDENT REPORTING

In the unfortunate case where an accident has happened, it's important for all concerned that the issues surrounding the accident are recorded for reference purposes.

Accidents, no matter how minor, should be recorded into an Accident Report Book or Form. Serious accidents must be reported to the Health and Safety Executive, who will investigate further.

 THINGS TO DO AND THINK ABOUT

Your school is a workplace just like any other. Write a list of hazards that could occur in your school and what you can do to combat them.

ONLINE

Head to www.brightredbooks.net/N5AdminIT to see an example of an Accident Report Form.

DON'T FORGET

Health and safety is a legal obligation enforced by the Health and Safety Executive (HSE): www.hse.gov.uk

ONLINE TEST

Test yourself on 'Health and Safety' at www.brightredbooks.net/N5AdminIT

ONLINE

Follow the link at www.brightredbooks.net/N5AdminIT for a link to videos on all types of health and safety.

ONLINE

Get clued up on what a company needs to do to keep within Health and Safety legislation at www.brightredbooks.net/N5AdminIT

HEALTH AND SAFETY: CURRENT LEGISLATION

In addition to the Health and Safety at Work Act (HASWA) 1974, students are required to have knowledge of the following regulations that impact on Health and Safety.

RESPONSIBILITIES OF THE EMPLOYER AND EMPLOYEE

Employers' responsibilities	Employees' responsibilities
Ensure work area has been assessed and risks are reduced.	Take care to avoid hazards in the workplace and advise their employers of any concerns.
Provide information and training.	Make personal adjustments to seating and screens to ensure correct posture and comfort.
Provide adjustable seating.	Ensure training sessions are attended and keep up-to-date on changes to Health and Safety regulations.
Ensure screens are both adjustable and able to tilt.	
Ensure employees are allowed breaks or time away from their workstation.	
Provide eye examinations if requested.	

ONLINE

Read more about RSI on the NHS website by following the link at www.brightredbooks.net/N5AdminIT

HEALTH AND SAFETY (DISPLAY SCREEN EQUIPMENT) REGULATIONS 1992

With more and more businesses using ICT in the workplace, this regulation was created to try and minimise the risks associated with the use of display screen equipment sometimes known also as Visual Display Units (monitors).

Some of these potential risks could be:

- eye strain
- back pain/ache
- repetitive strain injury (RSI)
- headaches

WHAT IS REPETITIVE STRAIN INJURY (RSI)?

This is a term used to describe pain in the muscles, tendons and nerves. It is often caused by tasks of a repetitive nature such as using a keyboard, by poor posture or by incorrect positioning of seating.

HEALTH AND SAFETY (FIRST AID) REGULATIONS 1981

'The Health and Safety (First-Aid) Regulations 1981 require employers to provide adequate and appropriate equipment, facilities and personnel to ensure their employees receive immediate attention if they are injured or taken ill at work. These Regulations apply to all workplaces including those with less than five employees and to the self-employed.'

Taken from HSE.gov.uk

GUIDANCE ON FIRST AID PROCEDURES

Employee welfare

First aid

First aid

The Health and Safety (First aid) Regulations 1981 require employers to provide equipment, facilities and personnel to enable first aid to be given to employees if they are injured or become ill at work.

In order to assess what is needed employers must carry out an assessment of what first aid needs are within the workplace.

The minimum provision of first aid on any work site is:

- a suitably stocked first aid box
- an appointed person to take responsibility for first aid arrangements including re-stocking the first aid box.

To be a qualified first aider you must take an approved Health and Safety Executive three-day training course. Individuals who are responsible for first aid in the workplace should only administer first aid appropriate to their level of training.

A list of approved training organisations is available on the HSE website.

First aid arrangements must be available at all times when people are at work, including outwith normal working hours. For example, shift workers must be considered in your first aid assessment.

The Health and Safety Executive First Aid Page (http://www.hse.gov.uk/firstaid/) provides further information on first aid and how to comply with the law.

Adapted from: http://www.hse.gov.uk/firstaid/legislation.htm/

FIRE PRECAUTIONS (PLACES OF WORK) REGULATIONS 1995

Employers are required to have procedures in place to meet the requirements of this legislation.

Employers are required to:

- adequately assess any fire risks to the organisation and to regularly re-assess these risks
- provide fire-fighting equipment and to ensure it is maintained through regular checks
- install and use warning systems
- train staff in fire evacuation procedures
- ensure that fire routes and doors are clearly labelled and unobstructed at all times
- carry out regular drills and tests of the warning systems.

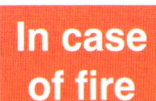

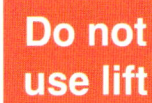

 **ONLINE TEST**

Test yourself on this topic at www.brightredbooks.net/N5AdminIT

THINGS TO DO AND THINK ABOUT

Look out for the fire evacuation posters in your school. When does the school test their fire warning systems?

SECURITY OF PEOPLE, PROPERTY AND INFORMATION

KEY ORGANISATIONAL RESPONSIBILITES IN TERMS OF PEOPLE, PROPERTY AND INFORMATION

Organisations not only need to consider the health and wellbeing of their employees – they also need to ensure that employees feel safe and secure at work.

Security measures should be taken to ensure that:

- staff and visitors feel safe and secure
- property is secure and theft is minimised
- both electronic and paper-based information is securely held and that confidentiality is maintained

SECURITY OF PEOPLE

The following security measures could be taken to ensure that staff and visitors feel safe:

Security staff on the door	Ensure that entrances are manned by security staff and visitors to the building are prevented from immediate access to the building.
ID badges to show that they are members of staff	Issue all authorised building users with an ID pass, which they should wear at all times. Issue visitors to the building with a visitor badge, which should be clearly displayed during the visit.
Swipe cards or PIN codes to open doors	Use swipe cards and PIN access for secure areas of the building to ensure the security of the content or staff within those areas.
CCTV cameras at entrances and exits	Install CCTV cameras to provide continuous recordings of those entering and exiting the building – especially outwith normal working hours.
Panic alarms	Install panic alarms – they can provide reassurance to staff who are working alone or in isolated areas.
Mobile phones	Issue employees with mobile phones to allow them to communicate in emergencies, or in areas that don't have landline connection.

SECURITY OF PROPERTY

The following security measures could be used to ensure that the building and property are kept secure:

Inventory of equipment and stock	Keep inventories of all company equipment with a description and appropriate serial numbers. This can help identify when equipment is missing and help the police to recover it.
Security marking equipment and property	Score equipment or mark it with ultraviolet ink to show that it belongs to the company.
Locked doors and windows.	Doors and windows should be locked when the building is not in use.
CCTV	Security cameras within the building to monitor secure areas such as Stockrooms.

SECURITY OF INFORMATION

The following security measures could be taken to ensure the safe handling and confidentiality of information:

Regular IT backup	This is when all data on the computer's systems is copied on a regular basis and is stored in a separate building or on a cloud server.
Passwords	All staff must have user IDs and passwords that are kept secure and changed on a regular basis.
Anti-virus software	Each computer should be protected by software that detects viruses, data loggers and other electronic dangers.
Locked filing cabinets	All paper files must be stored in fireproof lockable cabinets.
Fingerprint readers	These can be used to log-on to computer systems. The reader will only recognise the fingerprint of the individual whose computer it is.
Encryption	This is used to transfer sensitive data across the internet.
Non-portable drives	These could be used to stop staff downloading data and selling it to competitors.
Firewalls	These ensure that hackers cannot access the company computers.

CURRENT LEGISLATION

You need to know about the current legislative requirements affecting organisations which store data on paper or computers.

DATA PROTECTION ACT 1998

This Act states that organisations which hold personal data must ensure that the data is:

- held fairly and lawfully
- only used for the purpose registered with the Information Commissioner
- adequate, relevant and not excessive
- accurate
- not held for longer than is necessary
- held securely
- processed in line with the data subjects rights
- not transferred outside the EEA (European Economic Area).

COMPUTER MISUSE ACT 1990

This Act prohibits unlawful access to computer systems. It is illegal to:

- gain access to computer systems without permission
- gain access to computer systems with the intention of committing a criminal offence
- gain access to computer systems to change or alter details without permission
- make, provide and supply any materials or equipment that could be used to facilitate a computer misuse offence.

THINGS TO DO AND THINK ABOUT

Find out how it would affect a company if it lost its customer files.

KNOWLEDGE CHECK: PROVIDING AN ACCOUNT OF ADMINISTRATION IN THE WORKPLACE

HOW DO I MEET THIS OUTCOME?

For Outcome 1 of this Unit, you are required to:

1   Provide an account of administration in the workplace by:
   1.1   Describing tasks, skills and qualities of an administrative assistant
   1.2   Describing the key features of good customer care in the context of administration
   1.3   Describing the organisational responsibilities in terms of health and safety
   1.4   Describing the key organisational responsibilities in terms of security of people, property and information.

Use the checklists and tasks below to evaluate your learning from this Outcome.

DESCRIBING TASKS, SKILLS AND QUALITIES OF AN ADMINISTRATIVE ASSISTANT: SKILL SCAN

		Green light	Amber light	Red light
1.1	I can describe at least two tasks/duties of an Administrative Assistant.			
	I can describe at least two skills or qualities required of an Administrative Assistant.			
	I can explain the purpose of a Job Description.			
	I can explain the purpose of a Person Specification.			

Administrator wanted

We are looking for an enthusiastic and hardworking person to join our team. The successful applicant should have a background in Finance and must possess at least three National 5 passes. Two of these must be in English and Mathematics.

Duties

- Reception duties
- Filing and mail handling
- Event planning and travel booking

ACTIVITY

Test your knowledge on this area, by answering the following questions:

1   Using the extract to the left, name two other duties that you would expect to see in this advert.
2   Name one other document that could be sent to the applicants to provide further information about the job.
3   Outline three qualities expected of an Administrative Assistant.
4   'The Job Description is an important document in the recruitment process.' Explain this statement.

DESCRIBING THE KEY FEATURES OF GOOD CUSTOMER CARE IN THE CONTEXT OF ADMINISTRATION: SKILL SCAN

		Green light	Amber light	Red light
1.2	I can describe why customer care is important to an organisation.			
	I can list at least two benefits of providing excellent customer service.			
	I can list at least two consequences of poor customer service and describe the impact on the organisation .			

 **ACTIVIT**

Test your knowledge on this area, by answering the following questions:
1 Name three methods of market research that an organisation could use to find out how happy its customers are with the service they receive.
2 Outline the consequences of poor customer service to an organisation.
3 Describe three benefits of good customer service.

DESCRIBING THE ORGANISATIONAL RESPONSIBILITIES IN TERMS OF HEALTH AND SAFETY: SKILL SCAN

		Green light	Amber light	Red light
1.3	I can explain the purpose of Health and Safety legislation			
	I can describe what is meant by a 'hazard' in the workplace and provide some examples to illustrate this.			
	I can describe what induction training is and why it is important.			
	I can list the key information which must feature in an Accident Report form.			

 **ACTIVIT**

Test your knowledge on this area, by answering the following questions:
1 Outline two responsibilities of the employer with reference to the Health and Safety at Work Act 1974.
2 Explain the term Induction Training.
3 Justify the need for an Accident Report form.
4 Outline the responsibilities of the employee with reference to First Aid and Display Screen Equipment regulations.

DESCRIBING THE KEY ORGANISATIONAL RESPONSIBILITIES IN TERMS OF SECURITY OF PEOPLE, PROPERTY AND INFORMATION: SKILL SCAN

		Green light	Amber light	Red light
1.4	I can describe at least two security measures that organisations can implement to ensure the security and safety of people within the business.			
	I can describe at least two security measures that organisations can implement to ensure the security and safety of the property and the equipment within the property.			
	I can describe at least two security measures – both paper-based and electronic – that organisations can implement to ensure the security and safety of information.			

Caution
Wet floor

 **ACTIVIT**

Test your knowledge on this area, by answering the following questions:
1 Outline two methods of securing the following within the workplace:
   - property   - information   - people
2 Name three of the eight principles of the Data Protection Act.
3 Justify the importance of regularly changing your password.

 **ONLINE TEST**

Take the some of the short tests at www.brightredbooks.net/N5AdminIT

 ## THINGS TO DO AND THINK ABOUT

Review these checklists in preparation for your in-class assessments and before the end-of-course assessment. Remember that the end-of-course assessment:
- is practical
- is closed book
- uses your knowledge from this Unit.

ORGANISING AND SUPPORTING EVENTS

CARRYING OUT PLANNING TASKS

OUTCOME 2: AN OVERVIEW

For Outcome 2 of this Unit, you are required to:

2 Interpret a given brief and carry out administrative tasks in the context of organising and supporting an event by:

    2.1 Carrying out planning tasks, taking account of the budget available

    2.2 Preparing documents to support the event

    2.3 Carrying out follow-up activities

EVENTS

In the context of Administration and IT, an event is a planned assembly of people, brought together for a related purpose or cause.

Some examples of events are:

- meetings
- school events – concerts, dances, parents' information evenings, careers fairs, assemblies
- fund-raising events – coffee mornings, sponsored events
- interviews
- business trips
- promotional events
- product launches
- press conferences

Event planning has three key steps:

1 Planning – all tasks carried out **before** the event

2 Supporting – all tasks carried **during** the event

3 Follow up – all tasks carried out **after** the event

CARRYING OUT PLANNING TASKS, TAKING ACCOUNT OF THE BUDGET AVAILABLE

When planning an event, it is important to organise and keep track of all the tasks that need to be completed.

IMPORTANT PLANNING QUESTIONS

In the early stages of preparing for an event, important questions need to be addressed and answered:

1. What are the objectives of the event?
2. Where is the event going to be held?
3. When is the event going to be held?
4. How many people will be attending the event?
5. What is the budget for the event?

MEETING OF THE PLANNING TEAM

An initial meeting of the planning team can be held at this early stage, with meetings being held more regularly as the planning progresses.

Each meeting should have an Agenda and this will direct the meeting and keep those attending on task.

EXAMPLE:

Notice of Meeting and Agenda
A meeting of the Event Planning team will be held in the Seminar Room, on **Tuesday XXth April 20XX.**

AGENDA
1. Apologies for absence
2. Minutes of previous meeting
3. Matters arising
4. Purpose of event
5. Date of event
6. Proposed venues
7. Any other business
8. Date of next meeting

Rachel Lewis
Secretary

After each meeting, the secretary will prepare the minutes of the meeting and send these to each person attending the meeting. He/she can also e-mail the date of the next meeting to those involved in the group.

THINGS TO DO AND THINK ABOUT

Plan an event for charity at your school. What would you need to consider to run this event? Prepare an agenda for this event – what points would need to be discussed?

ONLINE

A sample copy of minutes of a meeting can be found on the online content section of the Digital Zone at www.brightredbooks.net/N5AdminIT

ONLINE TEST

Take a test on this topic at www.brightredbooks.net/N5AdminIT

DON'T FORGET

All meetings should be recorded – an Agenda keeps those attending on task during the meeting and the Minutes record what has been said and what has been agreed. This is useful as a record, but also for those who were unable to attend.

TO-DO/PRIORITIES LISTS AND PLANNING TOOLS

If you are involved in the role of planning an event, you might also have additional tasks to complete. The information below will suggest how you can manage these tasks.

TO-DO LISTS

A 'to-do' list will ensure that you keep track of all your tasks. This document simply lists all of the tasks that have to be completed. To-do lists can belong to individuals, teams or departments.

> **EXAMPLE:**
>
> **Parents' Information Evening**
> **To-do list**
> - Invite S4 – S6 parents.
> - Book catering for event: fair-trade café.
> - Book the concourse between 4 pm and 7 pm.
> - Arrange for displays and literature from various agencies involved in PD programme.
> - Arrange with Service Support staff to have seating laid out after end of school day before the event.
> - Prepare an Itinerary of events for key staff for the running of the event.
> - Contact external company about providing sound system for event.
> - Ensure presence of Head Boy and Head Girl and House Captains to meet and greet guests.
> - Ensure technology required – laptop, internet connection and presenter tools are all available and in running order.

PRIORITIES LIST

This is a very similar document to a to-do list. It is a list of required tasks – only this time, they are prioritised by importance or by deadlines.

> **EXAMPLE:**
>
> **Parents' Information Evening**
> **Priorities list**
> 4 Invite S4 – S6 parents.
> 2 Book catering for event- fair-trade café.
> 1 Book the concourse between 4 pm and 7 pm.
> 6 Arrange for displays and literature from various agencies involved in PD programme.
> 7 Arrange with Service Support staff to have seating laid out after end of school day before the event.
> 5 Prepare an Itinerary of events for key staff for the running of the event.
> 3 Contact external company about providing sound system for event.
> 8 Ensure presence of Head Boy and Head Girl and House Captains to meet and greet guests.
> 9 Ensure technology required – laptop, internet connection and presenter tools are all available and in running order.

ONLINE

A template of a to-do list is available online for reference at www.brightredbooks.net/N5AdminIT

This document is designed to be flexible – as tasks change, their priority will change. During the event planning stage, the Administrator can refer back to this list to ensure that all tasks are being completed.

ELECTRONIC DIARY

An electronic diary (e-diary) is an electronic scheduling tool – not too dissimilar to your school planner/homework diary. It is normally linked to your e-mail account.

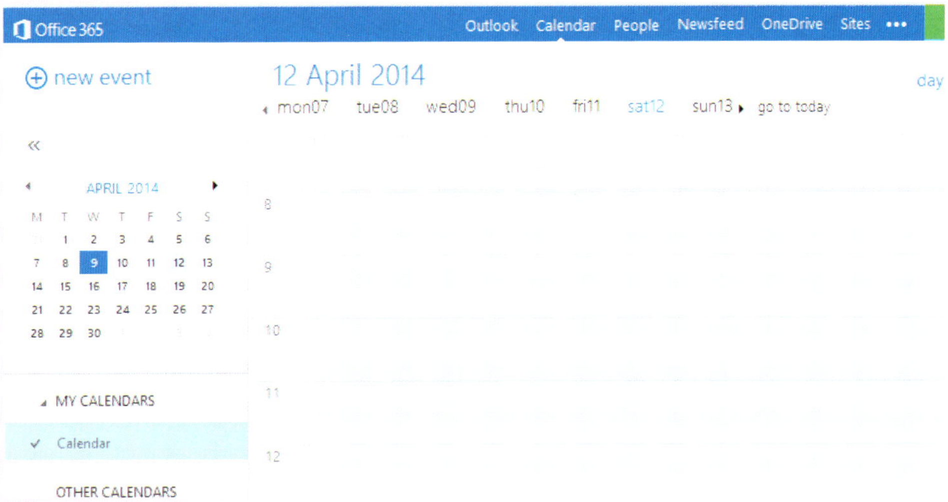

An e-diary is a useful planning tool because it allows the user to:

- create appointments and events in their diary and share these with others via e-mail
- set reminders

- attach documents to their appointment/ event requests
- share their diary with colleagues.

What should be entered in a new event?

- date and time of event
- location of event
- attendees

- importance
- any reminders
- key information about the event

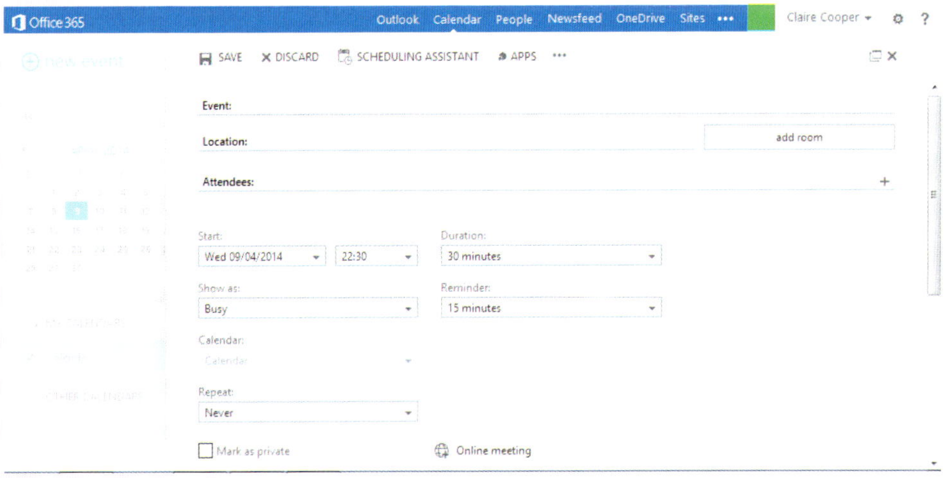

THINGS TO DO AND THINK ABOUT

Try using your e-diary to record when your school holidays are for the year.

FURTHER USEFUL PLANNING TOOLS AND BUDGETING

Before an event can take place, you'll need to gather information about the location, venue and transportation.

WEBSITES

There are several useful websites that you can use to source this information.

VENUE

Events can vary in scale, so researching a suitable venue can sometimes be difficult. Research the list of venues below and think about the events that could be held there.

SSE Hydro, Glasgow
http://thessehydro.com/default.aspx

Edinburgh International Conference Centre
www.eicc.co.uk/

Carnegie Conference Centre, Dunfermline
www.carnegieconferencecentre.co.uk/

West Park Conference Centre, Dundee
www.westpark.co.uk/

List of further Scottish venues
www.conventionscotland.com/content/default.asp

Medium to large venues
http://uk.hotels.com/

When choosing a venue, consider the number of people attending and the facilities that you will need:

- seating
- catering
- presentation tools – projector, ICT equipment and sound equipment
- WiFi
- parking

LOCATION

You could use the following websites to find out about the area the event is taking place in:

Google maps
www.google.co.uk/maps

AA
www.theaa.com/maps/index.jsp

Tourist Information
www.tourist-information-uk.com

When choosing the location of your event, consider the following factors:

- Where your attendees are travelling from.
- How central your location is – what public transport is available locally?
- Relevance – holding an event about Education in Edinburgh in Dundee would not be appropriate.

contd

TRANSPORTATION

You could use the following websites to find out about methods of transport or the route to the location:

AA Routeplanner (useful for planning a journey by road)
www.theaa.com/route-planner/index.jsp

The Trainline (useful for planning a journey by train)
www.thetrainline.com/

Skyscanner (useful for planning a journey by air, especially as it can identify which destinations travellers can fly to and from, from each airport)
www.skyscanner.net/

Expedia (useful for planning a journey by air, and also includes information about Eurostar.) www.expedia.co.uk/

When choosing the form of transport for your attendees, consider the following factors:

- Duration of the journey – start and end destinations
- Preference
- Budget
- Number of people travelling

DON'T FORGET

There is a section on Spreadsheets later on in this book (pp46-58).

ONLINE

Try the 'practise spreadsheet budgeting tasks' on the Digital Zone at www.brightredbooks.net/N5AdminIT

ONLINE TEST

Take the planning test at www.brightredbooks.net/N5AdminIT

THE BUDGET

Each event held will have a **budget** – a set amount of money that should cover the costs of the event.

A TV show called *Don't Tell the Bride* illustrates how a budget works. In this show, the groom is given a budget of £12,000 to plan and pay for all the elements of his wedding day – while the bride has no input at all.

A key feature of budgeting is a **resource list** – a list of resources needed for the event. Here's a sample resource list for a wedding.

BUDGETING SOFTWARE

There are many different types of spreadsheet software available to help you input and analyse financial information, including MS Excel, Numbers and Open Office. This software is therefore an ideal tool when you are creating a budget.

A	I	O
Vendors	**Total Cost**	**Paid By**
Caterer/Reception	17000	Bride's Family
Ceremony	1000	Bride's Family
Band	2000	Groom's Family
Photographer	1500	Groom's Family
Videographer	1200	Groom's Family
Florist	800	Bride's Family
Bakery	500	Personal
Clergy	500	Personal
Dresses	350	Bride's Family
Invitations	200	Bride's Family
Total Cost	25050	
Total Bride's Family	19350	
Total Groom's Family		
Total Personal		

Wedding Budget List – Budget £12,000

	Estimated	Actual	Over/under
Venue	£2000		
Dress	£1000		
Rings	£1000		
Catering	£2000		
Flowers	£500		
Cake	£500		
DJ/Music			

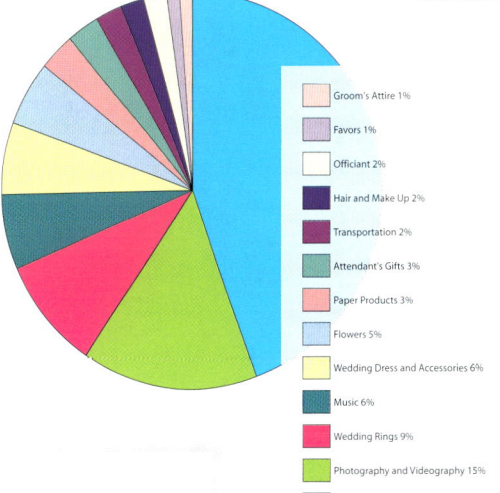

Groom's Attire 1%
Favors 1%
Officiant 2%
Hair and Make Up 2%
Transportation 2%
Attendant's Gifts 3%
Paper Products 3%
Flowers 5%
Wedding Dress and Accessories 6%
Music 6%
Wedding Rings 9%
Photography and Videography 15%
Reception 44%

THINGS TO DO AND THINK ABOUT

Look at the Wedding Budget List for the *Don't Tell the Bride* wedding above. Choose a venue for the wedding using some of the websites listed in this section. Is your choice over- or under-budget? How does this affect the budgets for the rest of the items on the list?

PREPARING DOCUMENTS TO SUPPORT THE EVENT

A key element of the Administration and IT course is the preparation of documents, using a variety of software packages. It is vital that you are able to recognise the best package for the task you are set.

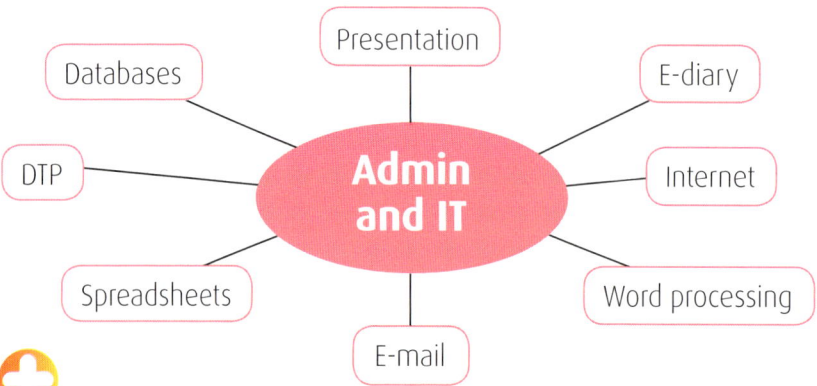

Admin and IT
- Presentation
- Databases
- E-diary
- DTP
- Internet
- Spreadsheets
- Word processing
- E-mail

DON'T FORGET

Databases have many uses. For a breakdown of how they are used in Administration and IT, turn to page 46–53.

DATABASES

You can use the tables function of database software to keep a record of attendees and a detailed list of venues and their facilities, and to record suppliers.

WORD PROCESSING

Word processing software is particularly useful for the following:

- business letters
- memoranda
- business reports
- to-do lists/priorities lists
- meeting documentation
- forms
- itineraries

DESK-TOP PUBLISHING (DTP)

DTP or desk-top publishing software is also used in event planning. The following items can be created using DTP software:

- name badges
- business cards
- posters/advertising materials
- newsletters
- leaflets
- certificates
- room layout plans

PRESENTATION

Presentation software is also used in event planning. For example, presentations can be used:

- during planning meetings to help direct the discussions
- by guest speakers at the event – so ensure that it is tested before the event
- to enable guests to learn more about the purpose of the event, or the background of the organisation.

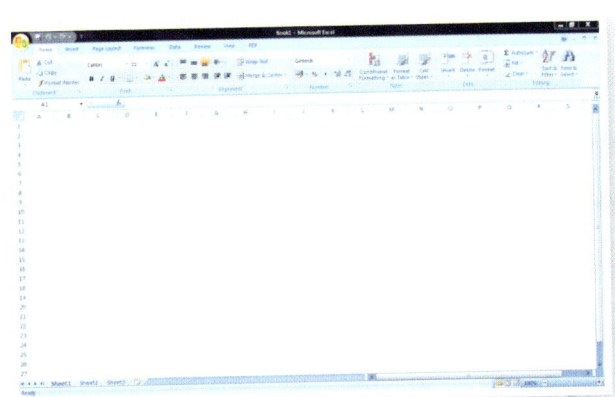

SPREADSHEETS

Spreadsheets can be used to prepare financial statements and budgets.

You can also use this software to create visual aids such as charts and graphs that you can use in the planning meetings or during the event itself.

E-MAIL

You can use e-mail in all the key stages of event. It is a vital tool that you can use to communicate with everyone involved in the event, from planners to suppliers and guests. You can also use e-mail to send and receive documents that will be used at the event.

DON'T FORGET

Turn to page 54 for more information about word processing.

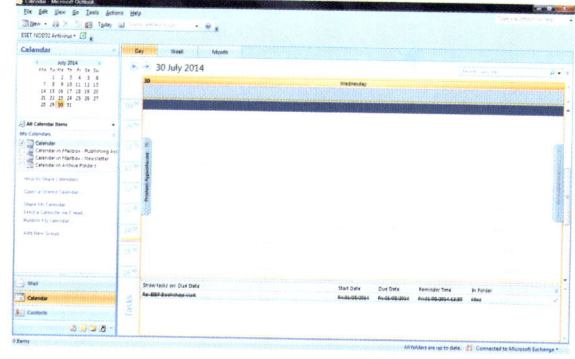

E-DIARY

The e-diary function will help you to keep track of important dates, times of meetings and tasks with deadlines. Everyone in the team can share their e-diaries, so you can all see when everyone is free to meet.

INTERNET

Using the internet to carry out desk research is an important skill for an Administration and IT candidate. When planning an event, you can use the internet to search for information on venues, location, transport, suppliers, catering and much more.

ONLINE

Templates for several of these documents can be found on our Digital Zone at www.brightredbooks.net/N5AdminIT

ONLINE TEST

Test yourself on this topic at www.brightredbooks.net/N5AdminIT

THINGS TO DO AND THINK ABOUT

Think about the School Prom – what would be on the resource list? What software would you use to keep track of the planning?

CARRYING OUT FOLLOW-UP ACTIVITIES

An event doesn't finish once everyone has left the venue – the organisers have to complete several follow-up tasks to evaluate the success of the event and learn from their experiences.

EVALUATION FORM

ONLINE

Follow the links at www.brightredbooks.net/N5AdminIT for some examples of how to create online surveys.

An Administrator should be able to use an appropriate software package to produce an evaluation form for the delegates to complete.

You can design this form so that delegates can complete it online or in paper format.

Although the questions asked will depend on the event, here are some general sample questions that you could feature in an evaluation form.

'Closed' questions are sometimes better for an evaluation form, as you can limit the responses you get back and this is easier to summarise.

Sample evaluation form

	Strongly disagree				Strongly agree
	1	2	3	4	5
Venue: The venue was completely suitable for the event.					
Venue: The catering fulfilled my expectations.					
Venue: The venue was easy to find.					
Materials: The resources available at the event were completely appropriate.					
Event: The objectives of the event were clearly communicated.					
Event: The event was well organised and structured.					

FEEDBACK FORM

A feedback form is not the same as an evaluation form. With an evaluation form, you are trying to gather data on how the attendees found the venue, location, resources and the catering. With a feedback form, where you are trying to gather more qualitative information based on opinion and feelings, your questions will be 'open-ended'.

Evidence gathered from evaluation forms and feedback forms should be collated and used to improve future events. Spreadsheet software is a useful tool to use for this as it will allow you to display the results in the form of graphs and charts.

ScotRail SCOTLAND'S RAILWAY   Home   Tickets & Offers ▾   More ▾

Feedback Form

We really want to hear your comments about our services. Please complete the form below and tell us what you think.

Alternatively contact our Customer Relations Department:

Email: scotrailcustomer.relations@firstgroup.com
Tel: 0845 601 5929
ScotRail Customer Relations, PO BOX 7030, Fort William, PH33 6WX

Name: *

Telephone:

Email: *

Your Feedback: *

An ideal example of a customer feedback form on the ScotRail website.

WHY IT'S IMPORTANT TO EVALUATE OPINIONS AND GATHER FEEDBACK

It is very important that you take time to gather feedback and evaluate opinions so you can learn from the experience and improve your practice for future events.

It is important to address any issues of concern and feed this back to people who attended the event, so they feel that they have been heard and that their opinions matter to the organisation.

Bad publicity as a result of poor customer service or experiences can have a detrimental impact on the future success of a business.

The BBC's *Watchdog* programme is dedicated to highlighting customer concerns and bringing to light organisations that are not as customer-focused as they could or should be.

ACKNOWLEDGEMENTS DOCUMENTS

In addition to gathering feedback, it is also important to thank the participants for attending the event.

These responses will take different formats, depending on the formality of the event, and can include:

- e-mails
- cards
- letters
- newsletters

ONLINE

Find out more about the BBC show *Watchdog* at www.brightredbooks.net/N5AdminIT

ONLINE

There are practice tasks available at www.brightredbooks.net/N5AdminIT

DON'T FORGET

Further guidance on how to use spreadsheet software can be found on page 44.

THINGS TO DO AND THINK ABOUT

Design a feedback form for your school catering service. Which software package would you use? What information would you need?

ONLINE TEST

Take the test on this topic at www.brightredbooks.net/N5AdminIT

KNOWLEDGE CHECK: ORGANISING AND SUPPORTING EVENTS

HOW DO I MEET THIS OUTCOME?

For Outcome 2 of this Unit, you are required to:

2   Interpret a given brief and carry out administrative tasks in the context of organising and supporting an event by:

    2.1   Carrying out planning tasks, taking account of the budget available

    2.2   Preparing documents to support the event

    2.3   Carrying out follow-up activities

Use the checklists and tasks below to evaluate your learning from this Outcome.

CARRYING OUT PLANNING TASKS, TAKING ACCOUNT OF THE BUDGET AVAILABLE: SKILL SCAN

		Green light	Amber light	Red light
2.1	I can state examples of events.			
	I can create and prioritise a to-do list.			
	I can list the features of an e-diary.			
	I can list the factors that should be considered when planning an event.			
	I can describe what a budget is and explain why it is important to the planning of an event.			

 **ACTIVITY**

1. (a)   You have been asked to plan a school awards ceremony. Using the template to-do list on the website, list the tasks that you would have to complete to make the event happen.

    (b)   Prioritise this list, using the task list from part (a).

2.   Identify three features of an e-diary.

3.   You have to organise transportation for two members of staff who are travelling from Edinburgh to London for a training conference. They have a budget of £500 for their transport and accommodation for one night.

Accommodation Costs   £295

Transport – Plane/Train/Coach   £???

Overall cost   £ Must not exceed £500

If they were travelling on the date of your birthday this year, what would the cost of travelling by train be for these two people? What would it cost to fly, or travel by coach?

PREPARING DOCUMENTS TO SUPPORT THE EVENT: SKILL SCAN

		Green light	Amber light	Red light
2.2	I can name various software packages used by Administrators when planning an event.			
	I can identify which software package best suits a particular task.			
	I can recognise business documents from templates.			

ONLINE

Here's a practical assessment to help you prepare for this. All the files needed for this assessment can be found on our Digital Zone at www. brightredbooks.net/AdminIT

1 Your manager has asked you to prepare a draft of a certificate that will be used to recognise employees' achievements when completing training courses. Which software package would you use to do this and why?

2 Your manager is attending a meeting of the Board of Directors and would like to take along some charts detailing a comparison of this year's financial statements with last year's financial statements. What software package would you recommend they use for this task?

3 Outline the features of a database, and explain how these can be used when planning an event.

4 Identify the document below.

Lighthouse Productions

To: All Staff
From: Sandy Hawthorn
CC: Stacey Jack
Date: 30/07/2014
Re: Office Stationery

Please note the following update regarding ordering stationery for the office.

- All orders should be emailed to Stacey Jack by the last Thursday of the month
- We will order stationery on the last Wednesday of the month
- Our new supplier in Power Paper
- Stationery will be stored in the cupboard in the entrance hall

CARRYING OUT FOLLOW-UP ACTIVITIES: SKILL SCAN

		Green light	Amber light	Red light
2.3	I can identify an evaluation form and a feedback form.			
	I can explain the importance of these forms.			
	I can identify appropriate software which could be used to create these forms, and then collate the results.			
	I can list other documents which would be used to communicate with the attendees of the event.			

 **ONLINE TEST**

Take some of the short tests at www.brightredbooks.net/AdminIT

THINGS TO DO AND THINK ABOUT

1 Compare the use of an evaluation form and a feedback form.
2 Design a feedback form for your school office. Which software package would you use?
3 Identify three documents that an organisation could use to communicate with individuals who have attended an event.

USING A SPREADSHEET APPLICATION

USING THE SOFTWARE

ONLINE

If you have studied National 4 Administration and IT, you should already be familiar with this software. If you haven't, there are several useful video tutorials at: www.brightredbooks.net/ N5AdminIT

OUTCOME 1: AN OVERVIEW

For Outcome 1 of this Unit, you are required to:
1 Use a spreadsheet application, to interpret a given brief by:
    1.1 Creating, editing and applying advanced functions and formulae to a workbook
    1.2 Creating a suitable chart

SPREADSHEET SOFTWARE

The most commonly used spreadsheet software is Microsoft Excel and, in this study guide, the screenshots used are from Microsoft Excel 2013. There are many other spreadsheet packages available and most offer similar functionality and toolbars:

- iWork - Numbers
- Zoho - Sheet
- Google Docs- Sheets

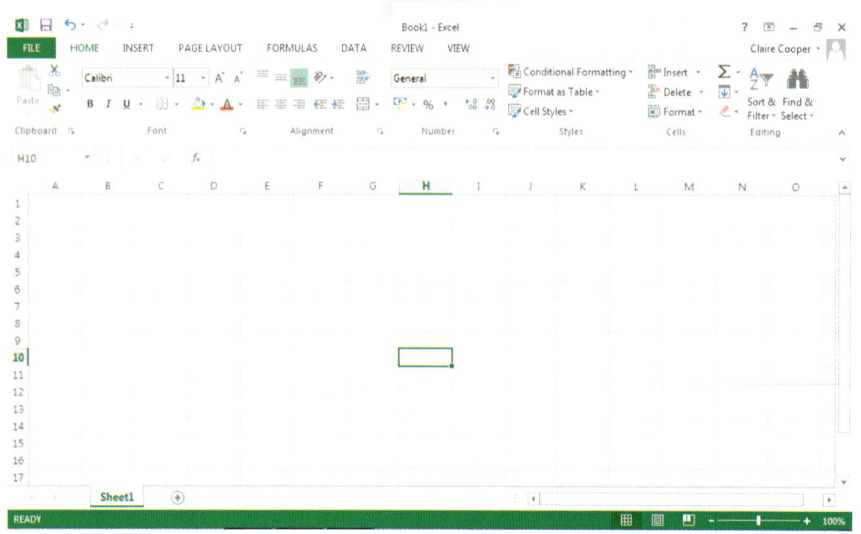

CREATING A WORKSHEET WITHIN A WORKBOOK

When you open up a new MS Excel spreadsheet, you should see a window similar to the one shown above. Each workbook will have at least one worksheet already visible. It will be named Sheet1. The name can be seen on the tab at the bottom of the worksheet.

These worksheets can be:
1 renamed
2 deleted
3 re-ordered
4 duplicated
5 and new sheets can be inserted

RENAMING SHEETS

To rename a worksheet, you can either double click on the existing name, or right click on the existing name.

If you choose to double click, this will highlight the existing name in black shading. You can then type over this name with one of your own choosing.

If you choose to right click, a menu will appear and you should select 'Rename' from the menu and then enter the new name for the worksheet.

DELETING A WORKSHEET

To delete a worksheet that you no longer require, right click on the Tab of the worksheet and choose 'Delete'. Be careful! You aren't given a warning message, so please make sure you are deleting the correct sheet.

RE-ORDERING WORKSHEETS

If you want to change the order of the worksheets, click on the Tab of the worksheet you want to move, hold down the mouse key and drag the tab to the new location.

contd

DUPLICATING WORKSHEETS

You might find it useful to duplicate a worksheet before you make any changes. To duplicate a worksheet:

- right click on the worksheet you want to duplicate
- choose 'Move' or 'Copy' from the menu
- tick the 'Create a Copy' radio button when the option window appears
- click 'OK'

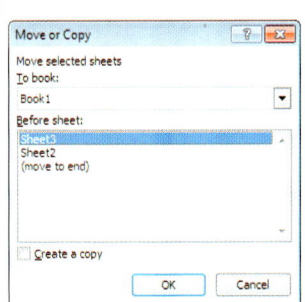

This should insert an exact duplicate of the original worksheet.

INSERTING NEW WORKSHEETS

If you need additional worksheets, click on the '+' which is located at the end of the existing worksheets.

This will simply insert an additional worksheet, which will automatically be located at the end of the existing worksheets. You can rename or re-locate these worksheets using the instructions above.

EDITING INFORMATION IN A WORKSHEET

Editing a worksheet can mean making changes to the contents of cells, the size of columns and rows and the presentation of the data.

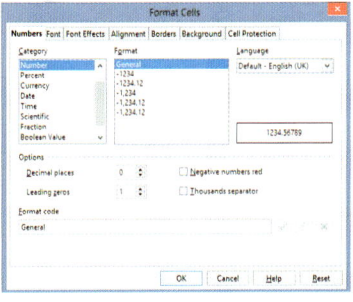

The Ribbon (or toolbar) has many options for editing the contents of a cell depending on what the cell contains. At this level of study, you can expect to see:

- Text
- Numbers
- Formulae

NUMBERS

Numbers can be formatted in a variety of ways. You can choose:

the number of decimal places shown	412.4, 412.40, 412.400
whether you want a comma for thousands	1024 or 1,024
how you want negative numbers to look	- 57 or -57
the currency symbol	£567 or $567
the way dates are written	4/4/67, 4th April 1967, 04/04/1967
to express the number as a percentage	12.5%
to express the number as a fraction	4/12 or 1/3

As before, highlight the cells with the data that you want to format – make sure that they are numbers – and then select the format type.

FORMULAE

Formulae will appear only when you choose to 'Show Formulae'. The contents of this cell will show 'Text' or 'Number' depending on what action the formulae have been used for.

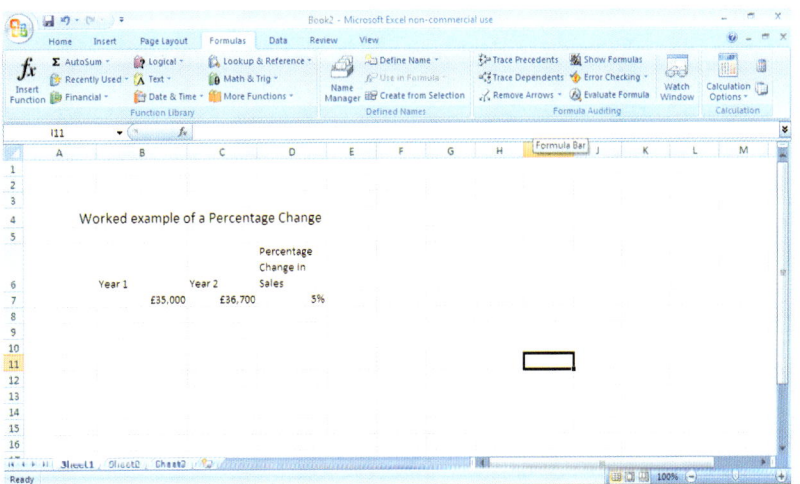

THINGS TO DO AND THINK ABOUT

Open up your spreadsheet package and familiarise yourself with the toolbars – find out how to perform some of the functions identified in this chapter.

HOME RIBBON

There are several formatting options available on the Home ribbon that will allow you to make the following changes:

- **Font** – change the font and how it appears
- **Alignment** – change the positioning of the contents of the cell
- **Number** – change how numbers appear in a cell
- **Styles** – change the contents of the cell contents and how the worksheet appears
- **Cells** – insert and delete cells and rows and format the contents of the cells.
- **Editing** – insert Functions, filter the contents of a worksheet, find and select or replace contents and autofill or clear contents in cells or worksheets.

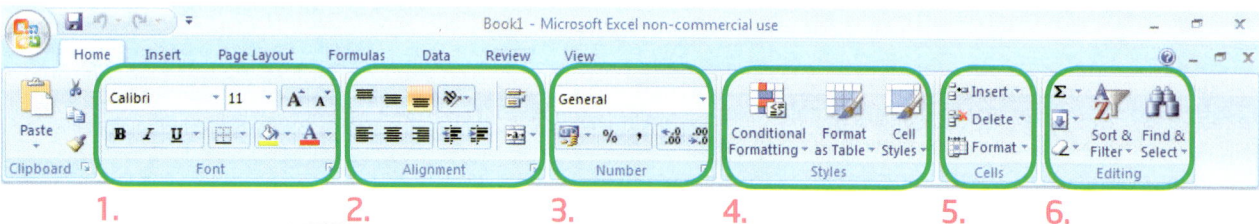

1.   2.   3.   4.   5.   6.

1. FONT CHANGES

You can make the following changes to the font within a cell:
- Change the **font** – for example, from Calibri to Century Gothic.
- Change the **size of the font** – for example, from size 11 to size 16.
- Change the **font style** – for example, to **Bold**, *Italics* or <u>Underline</u>
- Insert a **border** around cells or a range of cells.
- Change the **colour** of the font – for example, from black to blue.
- Change the **background colour** of the cell – for example, from white to yellow.

These toolbar options are common across the various Microsoft software packages. This means that you amend or change data in a Microsoft Excel spreadsheet in the same way that you amend or change data in a Microsoft word processed document – the toolbar options look and behave the same way.

DON'T FORGET

The ribbons are there to help you so make sure you know where the tools are that you might need to use.

2. ALIGNMENT CHANGES

Alignment refers to the position of the information in the cells. The most commonly used alignment tools are Left, Centre and Right. When you key in text, the software automatically aligns to the left. Numbers are automatically pre-set to align to the right-hand side.

You can also change the alignment of the contents of a cell in the following ways:
- **Position** the contents at the **Top**, **Middle** or **Bottom** of a cell.
- **Indent** the contents or **remove the indent**.
- **Wrap text** – when there is a lot of detailed content in a cell, this allows you to wrap the content so it can be seen clearly.
- **Orientation of contents** – you can rotate the contents diagonally or vertically.
- **Merge** and **Centre** – you can merge cells together to make one larger cell. This will combine the contents and centre the information into the middle of the new larger cell.

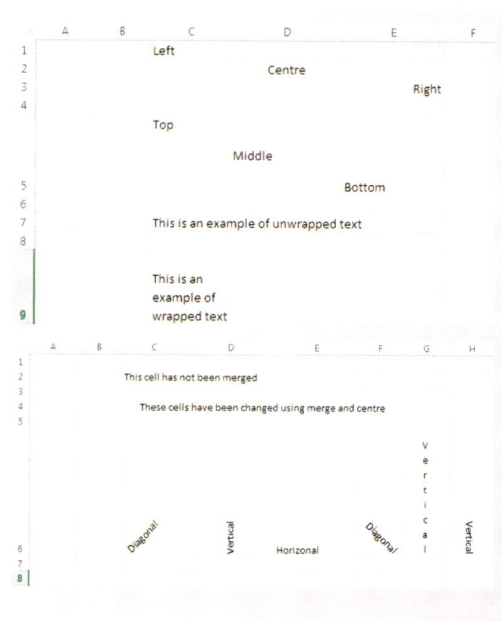

3. NUMBER

This section of the ribbon allows you to format a number entered into a cell, or a number that might have appeared as a result of a formula or function entered.

You can also change how the numbers appear in the cells:
- **Number Format** menu – allows you to choose the format for the cells – for example, Currency, Percentage or Time.
- **Accounting Number Format** – allows you to format for a particular currency – for example, Dollars or Euros.
- **Percent Style** – this is a quick shortcut to format a cell for percentage
- **Comma Style** – this is a quick shortcut to format with a 'thousands' separator
- **Increase and Decrease Decimal** – this is a quick shortcut to increase or decrease the number of decimal places in the number displayed in a cell.

4. STYLES

Conditional Formatting is used to change the **appearance** of the contents of the cell, depending on the **contents** of the cell.

Format as Table is used to display the contents of the spreadsheets as a table.

Cell Styles is used to create themes for the cells so that the content stands out.

These styles functions are not required at National 5 Administration and IT, but you can still make yourself aware of what they do, as they are useful functions of the software.

5. CELLS

This section allows the user to enter or delete cells, columns, rows and worksheets into the workbook.

The 'Format' option allows the user to:
- adjust the row, height and column width of cells
- hide and unhide cells
- rename sheets
- move or copy sheets
- change the Tab colour
- protect the sheet and lock cells

6. EDITING

You can use this area of the ribbon to do the following:
- **Insert a function** using the function shortcut: - **S**. (There is more detailed information on functions and formulae on page 35.)
- **Autofill** the contents of a range of cells if you are entering data that is related or part of a pattern. For example, enter Monday, Tuesday and Wednesday and Autofill will predict the pattern and enter the next few appropriate entries.
- **Sort** the contents of a range of cells, depending on set criteria.
- **Filter** the contents of a range of cells, depending on set criteria. (There is more detailed information on sorting on page 39.)
- The **Find and Select** option allows the user to find a particular value in a cell in the worksheet. This menu allows the user to replace entries – for example – changing the word 'School' to 'College' throughout the worksheet.

ONLINE TEST

How well have you learned this topic? Head to www.brightredbooks.net/N5AdminIT and take the test.

ONLINE

Check out the clip at www.brightredbooks.net/N5AdminIT to watch a tutorial on this.

THINGS TO DO AND THINK ABOUT

Recreate the following table using some of the tools that have been illustrated in this section. The changes numbered 1–3 below will help you.
1. Heading – has been 'merged and centred' and the font size has increased.
2. Sub-headings – have been 'Wrapped' and 'Centred and Middle Aligned' with 'Border'
3. Table data has been 'wrapped' in certain cells.

FORMULAE AND FUNCTIONS

Spreadsheet software is most commonly used for its business and financial applications. This software allows the user to perform complex calculations through the use of formulae and functions.

BASIC CALCULATIONS

The following operators are used in basic calculations:

- + Addition
- - Subtraction
- / Division
- * Multiplication

Addition +	=B5+B6	this adds the value in B5 to the value in B6
Subtraction -	=C6-C4	this subtracts the value in C4 from the value in C6
Division /	=D5/D1	this divides the value in D5 by the value in D1
Multiplication *	=C5*D2	this multiplies the value in C5 by the value in C2

While these operators are often used in basic calculations, they can also be used in quite complex, combined calculations, so it is important that you understand how to use them when you are constructing a formula.

All formulae and functions begin the same way. An equals (=) symbol must be entered first. This tells the software that you want to enter a formula or function.

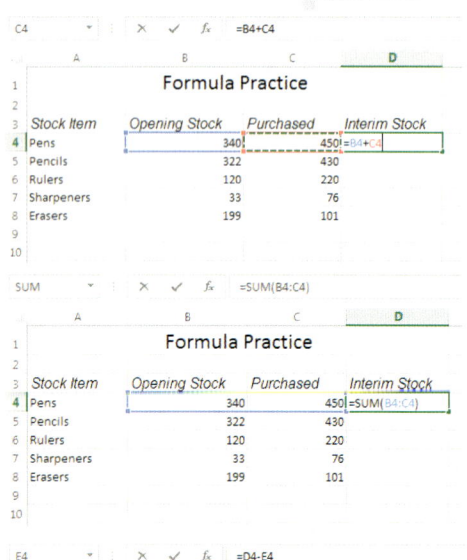

ADDITION/AUTOSUM

To add together the contents of cell references B4 and C4, you must first enter the equals (=) symbol to indicate to the software that you are performing a calculation.

The example shown illustrates an addition calculation that is carried out using the Autosum (S) function.

In this example, we have to add together the Opening Stock figure and the Purchased figure to calculate the Interim Stock figure.

By using the Autosum function, the equals (=) symbol is automatically entered and the software will also highlight the nearest cells to help you anticipate what you want to add.

SUBTRACTION

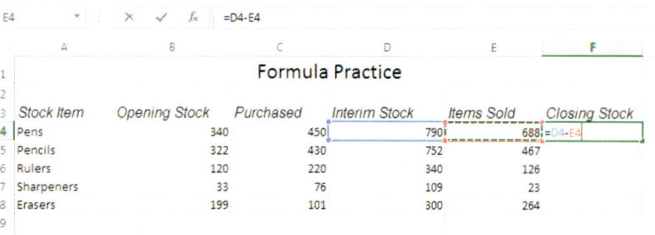

In this example, we have to deduct the number of items that have been sold from the number of items that had been held in stock. The result of this formula should be the Closing Stock figure.

As with both the Addition and the Autosum options, the calculation begins with an equals (=) symbol.

DIVISION

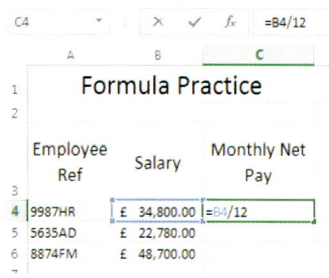

In this example, we are given the employee's annual salary amount and we must use a formula to work out what their monthly net pay would be. So we have to divide the salary by 12 (12 months in a year).

As with the previous example, the calculation begins with an equals (=) symbol.

MULTIPLICATION

In this example, we have to calculate the Stock Value. We therefore have to multiply the number of items in stock by the selling price.

As with the earlier examples, this formula begins with the equals (=) symbol so the software recognises that we are entering a formula.

FUNCTIONS

A function is a pre-set formula in spreadsheet software. We have already used a function – SUM – to add cell contents together.

Other functions you should already be familiar with are:

- AVERAGE
- MAX
- MIN
- COUNT (NUMBERS)

The AVERAGE function calculates the average of a range of cells:

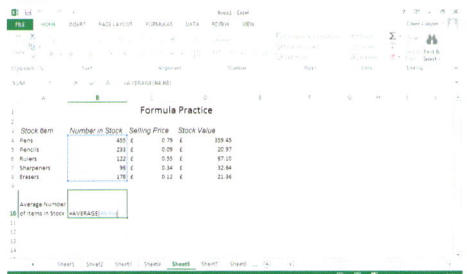

The MIN function analyses a range of cells to find the lowest value within the range:

The MAX function analyses a range of cells and identifies the highest number within the range.

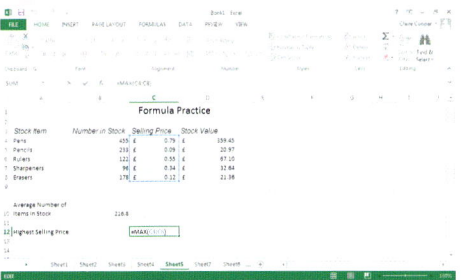

The COUNT (or COUNT NUMBERS in some versions) analyses the contents of cells that contain a numerical value and counts those cells that contain a value.

ONLINE

These formulae are required National 4 knowledge and skills. If you have not completed the National 4 course or would simply like some more practice on these types of calculations, please try the practice tasks at www.brightredbooks/N5AdminIT

THINGS TO DO AND THINK ABOUT
REFERENCING CELLS IN FORMULAE AND FUNCTIONS

In the example above, if we want to find out how many different stock items the business sells, we have to choose from cell references B4:B8, C4:C8 and D4:D8 because they contain numerical values. We can't use cells A4:A8 because the function doesn't recognise non-numerical content.

These functions are required N4 knowledge and skills. If you have not completed the National 4 course or would simply like some more practice using these types of functions, please try the practice tasks at www.brightredbooks/N5AdminIT

In the examples above, we have referred to cells using their 'cell reference' – that is, their column letter and their row number – A1, C4 and so on.

In some formulae and functions, we need to refer to cells that are in another worksheet or another part of the same worksheet. To do this, we use:

- Named Cells
- Absolute Cell Referencing

These terms are explained in the following sections.

ONLINE TEST

Want to test your knowledge of this topic? Head to www.brightredbooks.net/N5AdminIT

DON'T FORGET

Formulae and Functions are a key part of the course – make sure you practice how to use them!

NAMED CELLS, REFERENCED CELLS AND IF STATEMENTS

NAMED CELLS

Rather than having to remember the cell reference it is possible to name cells. So instead of remembering that G56 is the cell with the total profit you can name it 'total profit'.

To name a cell:
1 Click into the cell that you want to rename – in this example it would be cell B13.
2 Click on Formulas tab.
3 Click on Define Name.
4 A pre-selected name will be entered – in this case Standing_Charge. If you do not want to use the name the program has selected, you can key over the one entered. The only rules are:
   - The name must not have any spaces – note the underscore in Standing_Charge
   - The name must not have already been used anywhere else in the workbook (not just the worksheet).
5 If you want to change the name later, follow the instructions above and change it by over-typing the original name.
6 Note that the name was C13 in the screen above and is now Standing_Charge.

If we now apply the formula using the named cell, we get:

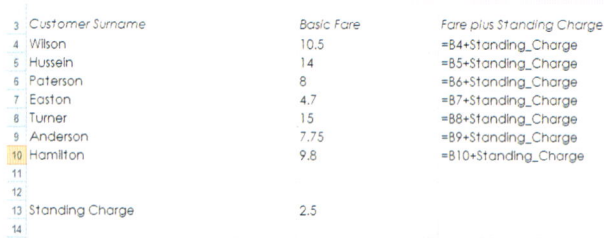

RELATIVE REFERENCING

There will be times when you want to apply a formula to all the cells in each row or column. This is called relative referencing and saves the user a great deal of work. Look at the example below, where the multiplication formula has been automatically applied across all the rows and columns.

Highlight the formula that you want to relatively reference, drag it down to where you want it to end and then select 'Fill Down'.

Stock	Cost/item	Value of stock
20	1.99	=B9*C9
34	2.5	=B10*C10
13	2.23	=B11*C11
56	2.45	=B12*C12
26	3.12	=B13*C13
13	5.23	=B14*C14
6	3.24	=B15*C15
33	5.14	=B16*C16
76	1.54	=B17*C17
34	2.55	=B18*C18

The 'Value of stock' column shows automatically altered values

ABSOLUTE REFERENCING

There will be times when you **don't** want the spreadsheet software to automatically apply the formula to all the cells in each row or column. Place dollar signs around the letter of the cell references you don't want changed.

ONLINE

You will see worked examples of both absolute cell referencing and named cells at www.brightredbooks.net/N5AdminIT

EXAMPLE:

Look at the example below, where we don't want the value of B4 to be applied when we copy it down.

VAT	20%		
Stock	Cost/item	Value of stock	VAT
20	1.99	=B9*C9	=$B$4*C9
34	2.5	=B10*C10	=$B$4*C10
13	2.23	=B11*C11	=$B$4*C11
56	2.45	=B12*C12	=$B$4*C12
26	3.12	=B13*C13	=$B$4*C13
13	5.23	=B14*C14	=$B$4*C14
6	3.24	=B15*C15	=$B$4*C15
33	5.14	=B16*C16	=$B$4*C16
76	1.54	=B17*C17	=$B$4*C17
34	2.55	=B18*C18	=$B$4*C18

IF STATEMENTS

As a National 5 candidate, you also need to know how to use an IF Statement. This function analyses the contents of a specific cell and enters a solution based on the criteria set.

To perform an analysis using an IF statement, click into the cell in which the answer is to be displayed and click on the FX function on the toolbar. Alternatively, click on the Formulas Tab and click on Insert Function. You will then see the window shown.

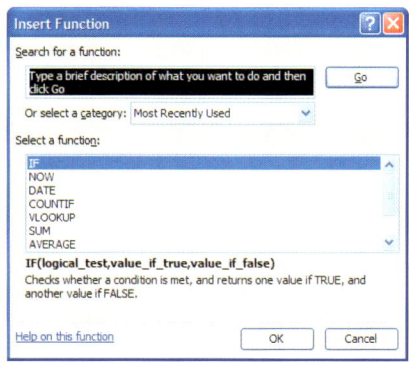

It is the first function listed, but if it isn't visible, type the word IF into the 'Search for a Function' box and find it that way. When you have highlighted IF click OK to move onto the next step. We have three sections to complete here:

1 Logical test   2 Value if true   3 Value if false

The **logical test** is the field that will feature the condition (the question you are asking the software to answer).

The Value if true will contain what we want to display if the condition is met.

The Value if false will contain what we want to display if the condition is not met.

WORKED EXAMPLES OF IF STATEMENTS

The **logical test** is the question you are asking the software to answer and this should be fairly obvious in the question presented to you.

EXAMPLE:

'If the Actual Sales value is higher than the Targeted Sales value, then enter the comment 'Reached Target', otherwise enter 'Not Reached'

So in this example, the logical test is:
'Is the value entered in cell reference B5 greater than the value entered in cell reference C5'
You would enter this into the function box as: B5>C5
The Value if true is 'Reached Target'
The Value if false is 'Not Reached'
As you are entering the information, you will see information appearing to the right-hand side of the white box.
Beside the Logical test box it says = TRUE because the software has recognised the answer needed here would be the Value if true.
The final formula result appears at the bottom of the box and allows you to check your answer before clicking on the OK button.

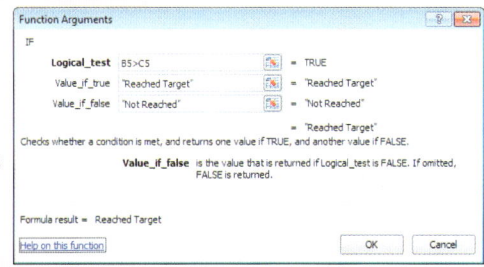

MORE HELP ON IF STATEMENTS

- **Logical tests** – these usually involve comparing the contents of one cell to a value provided or entered.

- **Value if true** – this can be presented as Text, a number or a formula. For example:
  - Target Not Reached   - £45   - =B4 * 110%

- **Value if false** – as with the 'Value if true', this can be entered as Text, a number or a formula. However, if you are not advised specifically what the Value if false is, then it you could leave this empty or enter a Zero (0). If you leave it blank, the software will enter the word FALSE.

THINGS TO DO AND THINK ABOUT

Try the practice tasks on IF Statements on the Digital Zone.

USING PERCENTAGES AND SORTING DATA

USING PERCENTAGES IN CALCULATIONS

You will probably use percentages in many of the tasks you carry out with spreadsheets. There are several different ways you can do this. Here are some examples.

CALCULATIONS WHERE YOU WANT TO DISPLAY A PERCENTAGE

EXAMPLE:

You have been asked to show your test mark as a percentage. Your result was 55/85.

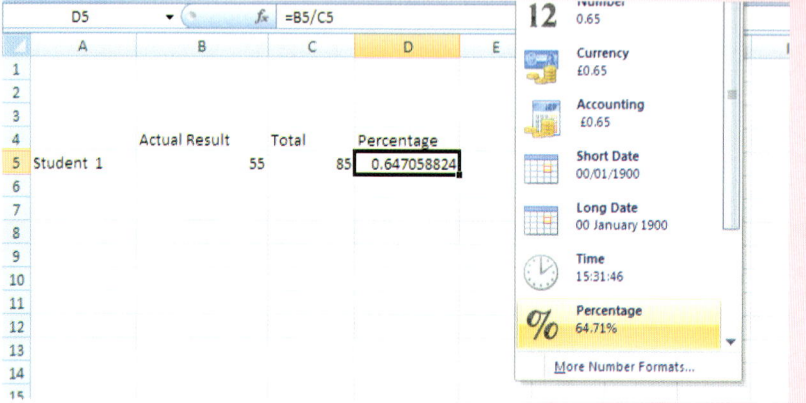

To show your mark as a percentage, use your formatting tools to change the number format to percentage. Your result was 64.71%.

CALCULATIONS WHERE YOU USE A PERCENTAGE TO WORK OUT A FIGURE

EXAMPLE:

You have been asked to calculate an employee's tax and national insurance payments, based on an annual salary of £15 000. Tax is calculated at 20 per cent and National Insurance is calculated at 12 per cent. The spreadsheet below shows how to set up this calculation.

Annual Salary	Net Monthly Salary	Tax	National Insurance	Gross Monthly Salary
15000	=C8/12	=D8*20%	=D8*12%	=D8-SUM(E8:F8)

CALCULATIONS WHERE YOU USE A PERCENTAGE TO SHOW AN INCREASE

EXAMPLE:

You have been asked to show a forecasted income statement for Cooper Bakery. The owner anticipates an increase of 3.4 per cent in income (currently £59 400) over the next four months. The spreadsheet below shows how to set up this calculation.

Income Statement for Cooper Bakery

Month 1 - Actual	Month 2 - Forecasted	Month 3 - Forecasted
59400	=B7+(B7*3.4%)	=C7+(C7*3.4%)

contd

CALCULATIONS WHERE YOU USE A PERCENTRAGE TO SHOW A DECREASE

EXAMPLE:

You have been asked to calculate a 4 per cent fall in sales, which are currently £45 000.

Income Statement for Cooper Bakery

Month 1 - Actual	Month 2 - Forecasted	Month 3 - Forecasted
45000	=B7-(B7*4%)	=C7-(C7*4%)

CALCULATIONS WHERE YOU HAVE TO SHOW THE DIFFERENCE BETWEEN TWO VALUES AS A PERCENTAGE (SOMETIMES REFERRED TO AS A PERCENTAGE CHANGE)

EXAMPLE:

Year 1 sales were £35 000 and Year 2 sales were £36 700: calculate the difference between these two values and display your answer as a percentage.

Worked example of a Percentage Change

Year 1	Year 2	Percentage Change in Sales
35000	36700	=(C7-B7)/B7

In this example, you would need to format your answer to display the final result as a percentage, in the same way you did in the first example.

Worked example of a Percentage Change

Year 1	Year 2	Percentage Change in Sales
£35,000	£36,700	5%

SORT DATA

You can sort a spreadsheet in a number of ways.

Select the Sort menu and choose from a number of options. You can sort by more than one column and you can sort by ascending or descending order:

- ascending means A to Z or 1 to 100 (and onwards)
- descending means Z to A or 100 to 1

Make sure you highlight the data that you want to sort. Note that this doesn't usually include the headings!

THINGS TO DO AND THINK ABOUT

Plan a menu for a special dinner. Use a spreadsheet to list the items you'd need to buy to cook the food, using formulae where appropriate. Set yourself a budget of £50.

DON'T FORGET

Remember to highlight the data you wish to sort before clicking on the 'Sort' option on the toolbar.

ONLINE

Head to www.brightredbooks.net/N5AdminIT to watch a clip about Excel.

ONLINE TEST

Take the topic test at www.brightredbooks.net/N5AdminIT

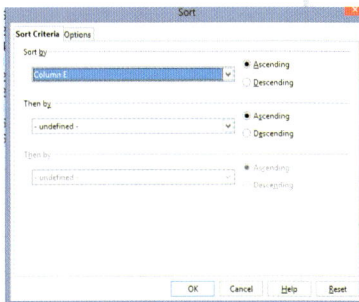

Sort data menu

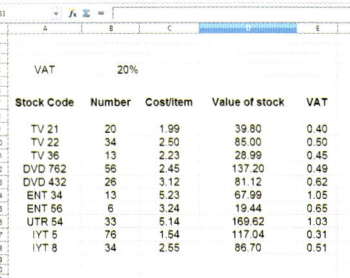

Unsorted data

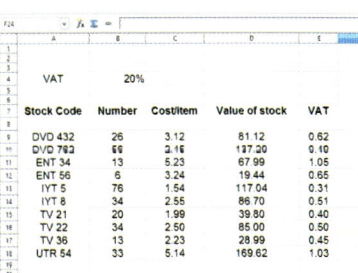

Sorted by column A into descending order

CHARTING

Charting is the graphic representation of numerical data. Charts can be used to present data in an format that is easy to read and interpret, and can also be used to highlight trends in the data.

Spreadsheets enable you to create a variety of charts from their data.

TYPES OF CHARTS

There are different types of charts available:

Pie Charts

Total Charge

■ Annie ■ Michael ■ Susan ■ Claire ■ Derek ■ Scott ■ Kate

Column Charts

■ Annie ■ Michael ■ Susan ■ Claire ■ Derek ■ Scott ■ Kate

Bar Charts

Total Charge

■ Kate ■ Scott ■ Derek ■ Claire ■ Susan ■ Michael ■ Annie

Line Charts

Total Charge

Annie Michael Susan Claire Derek Scott Kate

—— Total Charge

The type of chart you use will depend on how you want to present the data, and the audience you are presenting it to.

CHARTING: A STEP-BY-STEP GUIDE

We are going to use the Salary Calculations spreadsheet here to illustrate what you need to do.

STEP ONE

The first step is to select the data that you want to use. In this example, the first chart will show a comparison of the salaries of the employees, so the relevant data have been highlighted above.

STEP TWO

You then need to select the charting option from the Insert tab. This option does vary between different versions of MS Excel, but all of the variations of chart are still available. In Excel 2013, the menu appears like the picture shown.

STEP THREE

You then need to select 'Recommended Charts' to choose how you want your data to appear. The illustration here shows how the data would appear as a bar chart, a column chart and a pie chart:

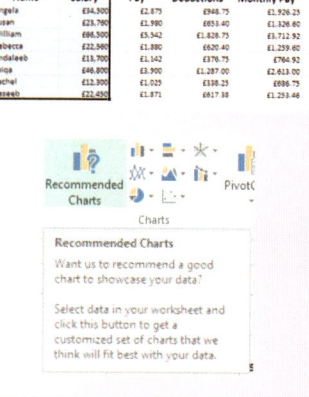

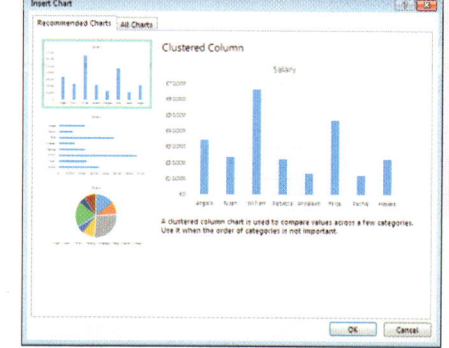

contd

STEP FOUR

Click on the chart type you want to use and then click on OK to create your chart.

STEP FIVE

The software will automatically insert your chart into the existing worksheet and will add an additional tab – Chart Tools – to the toolbar.

STEP SIX

This new Chart Tools tab consists of two sections: **Design** and **Format**.

- The **Design** section consists of tools that help you to change the way the chart is presented:
    - **Add Chart Element** – in this menu you can add labels to the axes of the chart, data labels and a legend
    - **Quick Layout** – this option allows you to change the presentation of the chart and move elements around
    - **Chart Styles** – this section allows you to format the chart and to add further detail avoiding the other menus
    - **Data** – this allows you to change the selection you have used to create your chart or to switch the rows and columns around to change the appearance of the chart.
    - **Change Chart Type** – this allows you to change your chart to another type – e.g. Column to Bar
    - **Move Chart** – this allows you to move your chart onto a separate worksheet. This is useful for printing.

- The **Format** section allows you to make formatting changes to your chart.

STEP SEVEN

Once you have completed your chart, you must remember to insert your name and details into a footer.

USING DATA FROM NON-ADJACENT CELLS

In some cases, the data you want to use will not be in cells adjacent to (or next to) each other.

To select cells that are not adjacent:
1. Highlight the first set of data.
2. Press and hold the CTRL key on the keyboard and then highlight the second set of data.
3. Follow steps 2 – 5 from the step-by-step guide above to create a chart based on this information.

Employee Name	Salary	Net Monthly Pay	Deductions	Gross Monthly Pay
Angela	£34,500	£2,875	£948.75	£1,926.25
Susan	£23,760	£1,980	£653.40	£1,326.60
William	£66,500	£5,542	£1,828.75	£3,712.92
Rebecca	£22,560	£1,880	£620.40	£1,259.60
Andaleeb	£13,700	£1,142	£376.75	£764.92
Faiqa	£46,800	£3,900	£1,287.00	£2,613.00
Rachel	£12,300	£1,025	£338.25	£686.75
Haseeb	£22,450	£1,871	£617.38	£1,253.46

THINGS TO DO AND THINK ABOUT

Use a spreadsheet task you have already completed and try to create a chart based on this information.

PRINTING

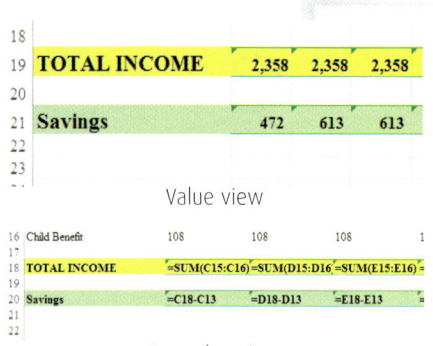

Value view

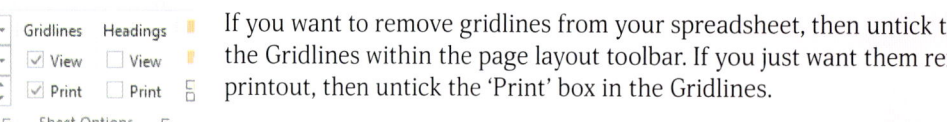

Formulae view

VALUE AND FORMULAE VIEW

Usually spreadsheets show the value view. This shows the value of any formulae that have been carried out on the spreadsheet.

You can change the view to show all the formulas that have been used in the spreadsheet. To change the view click on 'Formulas' then click on the 'Show Formulas' button on the Formula toolbar.

Formulae menu

PRINTING WITH OR WITHOUT GRIDLINES

Usually the gridlines that surround each cell are visible. You can print them with or without gridlines.

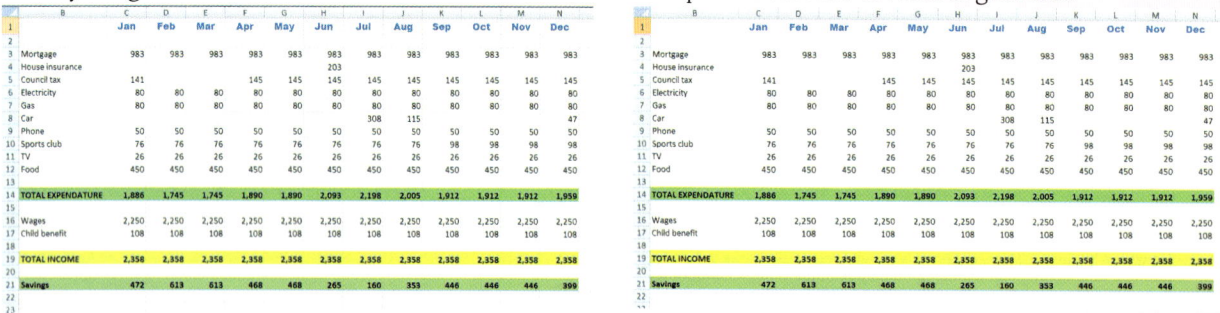

Spreadsheets with and without gridlines

If you want to remove gridlines from your spreadsheet, then untick the 'View' box in the Gridlines within the page layout toolbar. If you just want them removed from your printout, then untick the 'Print' box in the Gridlines.

PRINTING WITH OR WITHOUT ROW AND COLUMN HEADINGS

Sometime you might want to print out the columns and rows without the row and column headings (for example, A, B, C and 1, 2, 3).

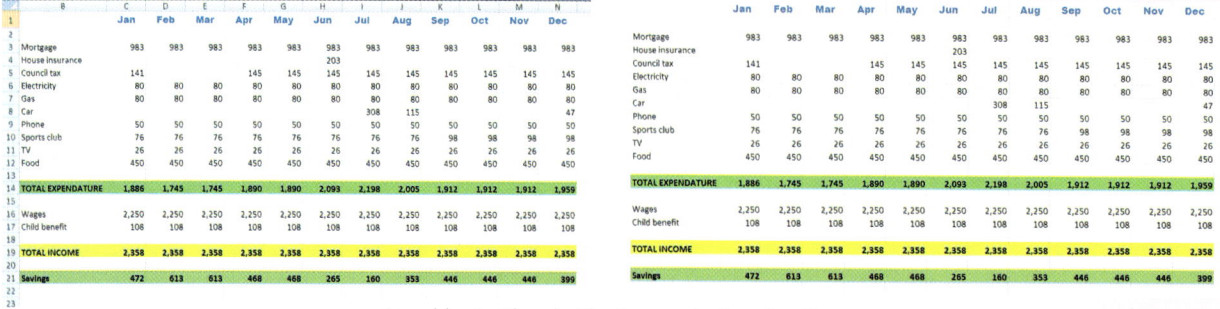

Spreadsheet with and without row and column headings

If you want to remove them from your spreadsheet, then untick the 'View' box in the Headings section within the page layout toolbar. If you just want them removed from your printout, then untick the 'Print' box in the Headings section.

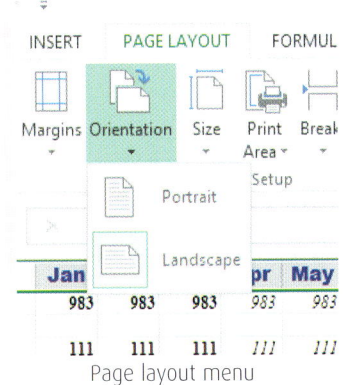

Page layout menu

PRINTING IN PORTRAIT OR LANDSCAPE

You make your page portrait or landscape just by clicking your preferred option from the Orientation menu on the page layout menu. The landscape option is usually preferred for spreadsheets.

PRINTING WITH HEADERS AND FOOTERS

If you want to print a header and/or footer on each page of your spreadsheet, then do the following:
- Select the Header/Footer menu from the Insert tab on the toolbar, and the following pop-up box will appear.
- Select a suggested Header or Footer from the pull-down menu or customise your own.

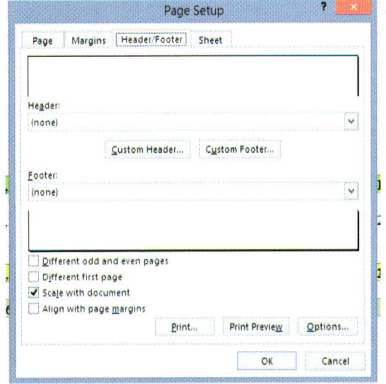

Page setup menu

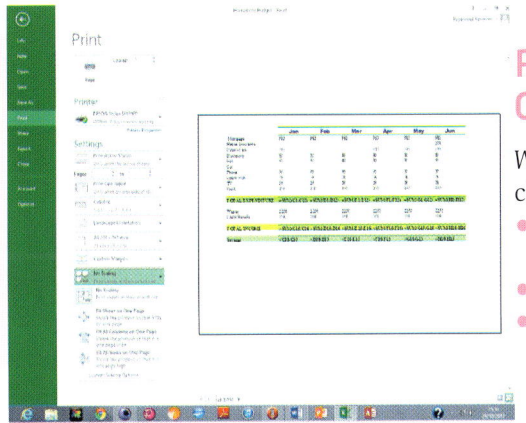

Print menu

PRINTING TO FIT ON ONE PAGE

When you decide to print, you can choose to do one of the following:
- Fit all of your spreadsheet onto one sheet of paper.
- Fit all the columns on one page.
- Fit all the rows on one page.

PRINTING A SECTION OF YOUR WORKSHEET

You can also select just a portion of your worksheet and print that on its own.

Highlight the area that you want to have printed, then click on 'Print' and select 'Print Selection' from the Print Active sheets menu.

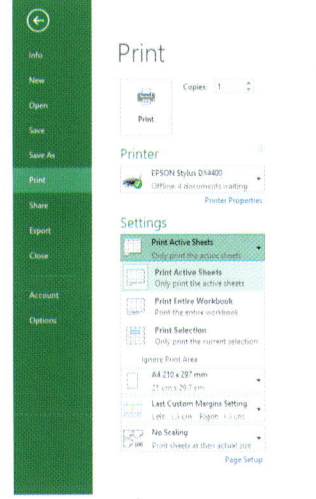

Printing a highlighted selection

ONLINE

Learn more about charting by watching the clip at www.brightredbooks.net/N5AdminIT

THINGS TO DO AND THINK ABOUT

Try the practice tasks on the website to see what you have learned from this chapter.

KNOWLEDGE CHECK: USING A SPREADSHEET APPLICATION

HOW DO I MEET THIS OUTCOME?

For Outcome 1 of this Unit, you are required to:

1 Use a spreadsheet application, to interpret a given brief by:

   1.1 Creating, editing and applying advanced functions and formulae to a workbook.

   1.2 Creating a suitable chart

Use the checklists and tasks below to evaluate your learning from this outcome.

CREATING, EDITING AND APPLYING ADVANCED FUNCTIONS AND FORMULAE TO A WORKBOOK: SKILL SCAN

		Green light	Amber light	Red light
1.1	I can create a workbook and use different worksheets by: • renaming a worksheet • deleting a worksheet • changing the order of a worksheet • duplicating a worksheet • inserting new worksheets.			
	I can edit information in a worksheet by: • recognising text, numbers and formulae in a worksheet • making changes to font, styles, alignment and number format.			
	I can use the following formulae and functions: • basic operators – Addition, Subtraction, Division and Multiplication • SUM, Average, MAX, MIN and COUNT • 'Rename a cell' reference and 'Absolute referencing' in formulae and functions • IF Statements • formulae to solve percentage-related calculations.			
	I can use the Sort function in spreadsheet software to: • sort data in ascending or descending order.			

ONLINE

Test your knowledge of this Outcome by attempting the spreadsheet tasks at www.brightredbooks.net/N5AdminIT

CREATING A SUITABLE CHART: SKILL SCAN

		Green light	Amber light	Red light
1.2	I can use the Charting function in spreadsheet software to: • recognise different types of chart and select the most suitable for the data presented • create charts from adjacent and non-adjacent columns of data • format the Chart Title and label the axes appropriately • print the chart on a separate sheet or embedded into the worksheet			
	I can print: • the entire worksheet • selections from the worksheet. I can print the worksheet: • in 'Value' view • in 'Formulae' view • with or without gridlines and row and column headings • in 'portrait' or 'landscape' view • on one page only			

DON'T FORGET

This is not a complete list – if you come across something you don't know, please ask your teacher.

BUSINESS TERMINOLOGY USED IN SPREADSHEET TASKS

While you are working through N5 Administration and IT, you will become familiar with some business terms that appear regularly in spreadsheet tasks. Some of these terms are listed below:

Term	Description
Quantity	This refers to the number of items held – sometimes used in the context of Stock or Sales. Quantity could be used in conjunction with Price to work out the Revenue or Total: = Quantity*Price Or it could be used to work out the total number of items held by the organisation: =QuantityJan+QuantityFeb+QuantityMar
Price	This refers to the value of an individual item – sometimes referred to as the Selling Price. Price is most commonly used in conjunction with a Quantity value to calculate Sales Revenue: = Price*Quantity It could also be used if calculating VAT: = Price * 20%
Revenue	Revenue is the term used to describe income generated from sales of goods and/or services by an organisation. It involves multiplying the quantity sold by the selling price.
Wages	This is the payment made to employees on a weekly, fortnightly or monthly basis. This is calculated by multiplying the number of hours worked by the rate of pay.
Salary	Some employees will be paid on the basis of an annual salary rather than on the basis of the hours they work. They normally have this annual amount paid in 12 equal instalments on a specific day or date of the month.
Income Tax	All UK citizens are required by law to pay Income Tax on their earnings through employment. This is deducted from the wages or salary payment and paid directly to UK Revenue and Customs. For accurate and up-to-date Income Tax bandings see: http://www.hmrc.gov.uk/rates/it.htm This is calculated as a percentage of Net Pay.
National Insurance	UK citizens pay a percentage of their earnings to cover National Insurance contributions, which entitle them to state benefits such as a state pension. To learn more about National Insurance visit: http://www.hmrc.gov.uk/ni/intro/basics.htm This is calculated as a percentage of Net Pay.
Net pay	This is the employee's wage or salary before any deductions. It is calculated either by dividing the Annual Salary amount by 12 or by multiplying the number of hours worked by the rate of pay.
Gross pay	This is the employee's wage or salary after deductions have been taken off. It is calculated by subtracting any deductions (such as Income Tax and National Insurance) from the Net Pay.
Bonus	This is an amount of money paid to an employee if they have met certain pre-defined criteria. A bonus is paid in addition to their wage or salary. It is normally calculated as a percentage of annual salary or earnings.
Commission	This is an amount of money paid to an employee if they have met sales targets. Commission is paid in addition to any wage/salary or bonus. It is normally calculated as a percentage of the overall Sales figures.
Discount	A discount is a deduction from another value. A Sales discount is when an organisation reduces the selling price to encourage more customers to buy.
Valued Added Tax (VAT)	This is a tax on most UK good and services. The current standard rate of VAT is 20%. To learn more about VAT visit: http://www.hmrc.gov.uk/vat/start/introduction.htm
Rate of pay Hourly rate Piece rate	These three terms all refer to the rate of pay an employee receives, depending on their employee contract. Rate of pay and hourly rate tend to refer to the amount a person is paid per hour of work, and in some cases this would be the National Minimum Wage. For an up-to-date figure for this visit: https://www.gov.uk/national-minimum-wage-rates Piece rate refers to the amount paid to an employee per finished item they have sold or produced.
Pension contributions	Pension contributions are classed as a deduction from earnings to contribute to pension payments made to the employee on retirement. These are normally calculated as a percentage of earnings/salary and will vary depending on the pension scheme that the employee is part of

THINGS TO DO AND THINK ABOUT

Refer back to this list when you are working through your practice tasks and you come across terms that you are unfamiliar with. If there is a term that you don't know or understand and it isn't on this list, ask your teacher.

USING A RELATIONAL DATABASE

USING THE SOFTWARE

OUTCOME 2: OVERVIEW

For Outcome 2 of this Unit, you are required to:

1 Use advanced functions of a relational database to interpret a given brief by:
  2.1 Populating a database, using forms
  2.2 Editing a database
  2.3 Manipulating information in a simple relational database
  2.4 Presenting information in a report, to a professional standard

Database software was designed to store large amounts of data electronically. The data stored can then be accessed by different users and presented in different ways. In this study guide the screen shots used are from Microsoft Access, although there are other software brands available, including:

- Filemaker Pro
- OpenOffice Base
- LibreOffice Base

VIDEO LINK

If you are not familiar with how to perform the tasks in this section, the videos at www.brightredbooks.net/N5AdminIT will help to guide you through these initial stages.

PRIOR KNOWLEDGE

As a National 5 Administration and IT candidate, you are expected to know how to create a table and a basic search (query) in a database.

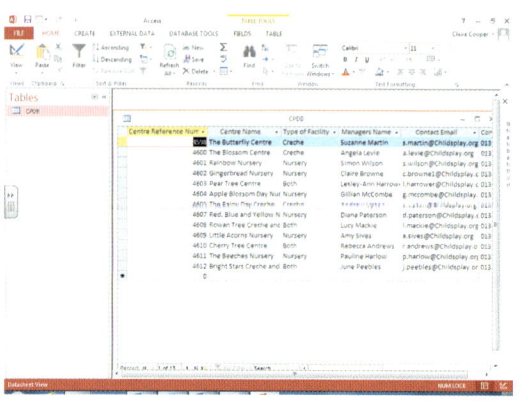

Datasheet view – this is when we can see all of the records

USING AND EDITING TABLES IN A DATABASE

A table is a list of all the records entered into the database. You can enter information into a table by:

- keying directly into the table
- creating a form and using this to enter information into a table.

In Access 2013, your table will appear in a similar format to that displayed in the screen shots. As with Microsoft Excel, Microsoft Access has ribbons instead of menus. The home ribbon is very similar, apart from the first section, which is called 'View'. This allows you to look at data in two ways:

- Design view, where you can see the Field Names and Data Types
- Datasheet view, where you can see all the records

DESIGN VIEW

In this view, you can enter and edit the names of your field and edit the format of the data types.

The data types that are commonly used in Administration and IT are:

- **Short text** – used for entering text into a field – for example Name, Address.

- **Number** – for entering numerical values into a field – for example Age, Number in Stock.

- **Date/Time** – this can be used for entering dates or times. You need to use the Format option under the General tab to choose how to present your Date or Time entry.

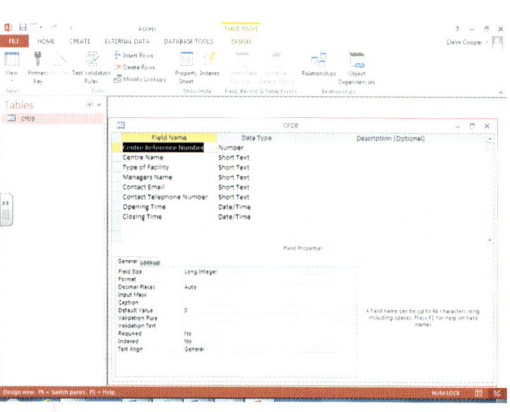

Design view – this is when we can see the Field Names and Data Types.

contd

- **Currency** – this is used for entering currency values. You can use the Format option to change the currency symbol or to change the decimal places.

- **Yes/No** – this is used to enter values that are fixed. Normally, a box will be visible in table or form view, and the user will tick the box to indicate a 'Yes' option and leave it unticked to indicate 'No'.

> **BEWARE:** At National 5 Administration and IT you will mostly use tables that have been created for your use, but if you are creating a new table, be aware that the software (Access 2013) will now automatically assign an Autonumber field and set this as a Primary Key.
>
> An Autonumber field is used to set a unique number for the record, and setting this as Primary Key ensures that no two records in the same table can have the same reference number. This is a feature that is used in business to set reference numbers for customers or users of their service.

DON'T FORGET

A telephone number should be formatted to 'Short Text' and not 'Number' as most numbers begin with a '0' and MS Access doesn't recognise this as a 'true' number.

EXAMPLE:

All Scottish students are registered with the SQA for examination purposes and are assigned an SQA number. No two students have the same number. If you needed to contact them to find out your results or to change your details, they will ask you for this number so it is easier for them to find your details. There is more information on primary keys in the section on Relational Databases (p49).

ONLINE TEST

Test yourself on this topic online at www. brightredbooks.net/ N5AdminIT

DATASHEET VIEW

In this view, the records will appear in tabular format. This allows the user to see all of the records at the same time.

In this view, you have access to two additional tool bars under the Table Tools ribbon:

- **Fields:** The options here allow you to edit the format of the fields.
- **Tables:** The only option we will use here is 'Relationships'. We will look at this in more detail on page 49.

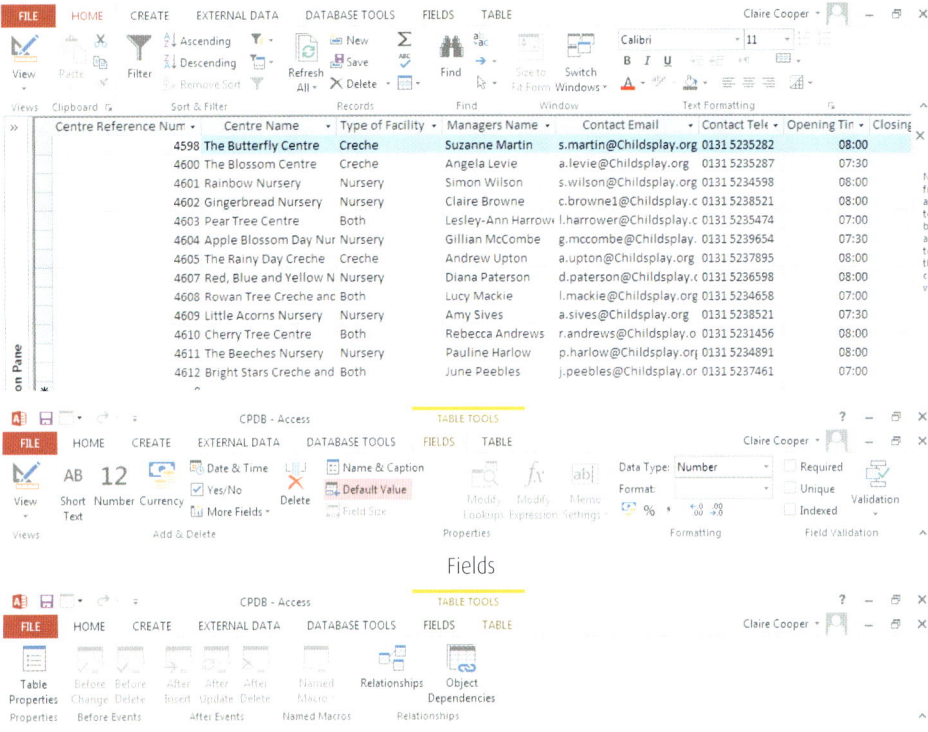

Fields

Tables

THINGS TO DO AND THINK ABOUT

Another example of an Autonumber field set as a Primary Field is National Insurance numbers. All UK citizens are issued with a National Insurance number when they become eligible to work. This number is used to hold their tax and national insurance details over their working life. It also tells employers that they are eligible to work. If you needed to contact HM Revenue & Customs (HMRC) they would ask you for this unique combination of numbers and letters to find your records.

Can you think of another example?

DON'T FORGET

When you are creating a new table, the software (Access 2013) will automatically assign an Autonumber field and set this as a Primary Key.

CREATING FORMS AND RELATIONAL DATABASES

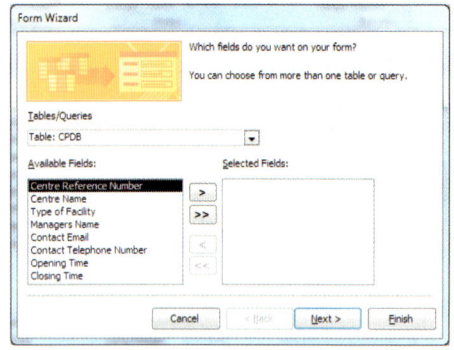

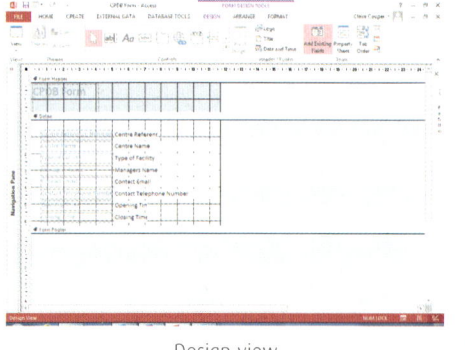

Design view

CREATING FORMS IN A DATABASE

Forms are used to make the process of entering data easier to do. You can customise the format and appearance of the form and add in any additional text to aid the user(s) of the form.

To create a form based on an existing table follow these steps:

1. Click on the Create ribbon and click on the Form Wizard option.

2. The window shown should open.

3. If you have more than one table in your database, ensure that you select the correct table.

4. Use the arrows to move the fields you wish to use from the Available fields to the Selected fields.

5. Then click on Next>

6. You are then asked to choose a layout for the form. We use Columnar here, but you can try out the others to see how they change the look of the form.

7. Click Next>. In the last window, you are asked to choose a name for the form.

8. Click Finish and your form should open.

9. It is important to remember that any entries or changes you make to the form will change the data in the table too.

10. To insert text or to change the appearance of the form, you can move to Design view. In this view you can:
   - change the name and appearance of the title of the form
   - add in an appropriate graphic
   - change the layout of the fields and change the formatting of the fields
   - add in a form and page footer.

USING FORMS TO INSERT DATA INTO A TABLE

Use the tools that appear near the bottom of the screen to insert new data:

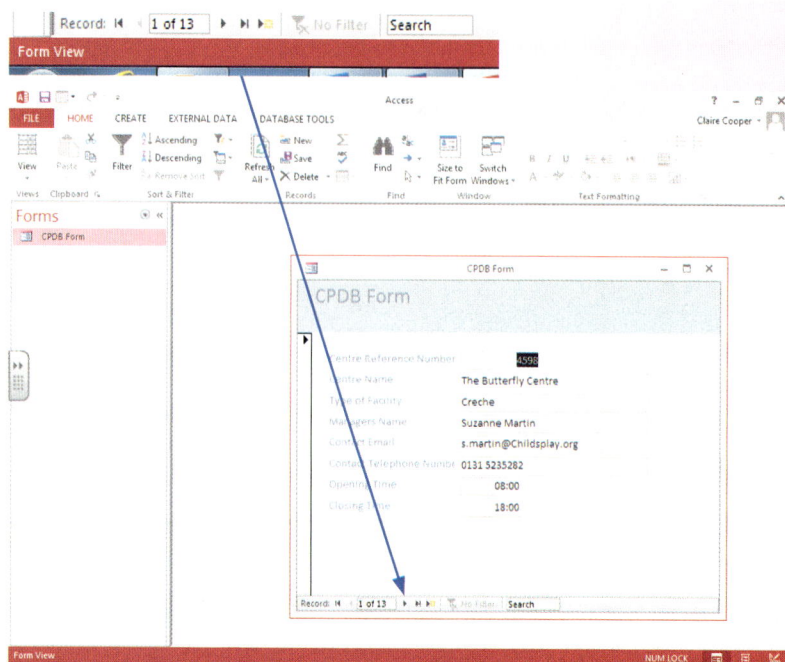

VIDEO LINK

To learn more about the Design view of forms, watch the short video at www.brightredbooks.net/N5AdminIT

RELATIONAL DATABASES

RELATIONSHIPS

A relationship is a way of linking information between two tables. You create a relationship by matching fields – usually with the same name – in the different tables. The types of relationship are:

- **One to One** – each record in a table relates to one record in another table.
- **One to Many** – each record in a table relates to one or more records in another table.

When using tables that are linked in a database, you must create a formal relationship between them using the fields in those tables. Recognising and using Primary and Foreign Keys is very important here:

- A **Primary Key** is a field that contains information that is unique to the record it is attached to. Examples include Customer Reference Number, National Insurance Number and SQA Number.
- A **Foreign Key** is a field that is used to link tables together when creating relationships.

DON'T FORGET

Referential Integrity refers to the link between a Foreign Key in one table and its links to other tables. If you choose 'Enforce Referential Integrity' you are alerted if you try to delete a record that has links to another table.

ONLINE TEST

Head to www. brightredbooks.net/ N5AdminIT to test yourself on this topic.

 THINGS TO DO AND THINK ABOUT

It's likely that the relationships will already be established in the tasks you are completing. However, it's useful for you to know how to create a relationship:

1. Ensure that each table has assigned Primary Keys.
2. Ensure that there is at least one common field.
3. Click on the Database Tools ribbon.
4. Click on the Relationships option button.
5. Click on Show Table and add your tables.
6. You should now be able to see all of the field names in each of the tables you have chosen to add. The Primary Key fields are indicated by the key symbol ( ) beside their name.
7. In this example, we have two different Primary Keys – but the field Centre Reference Number in the Centre Details table is also used in the Children table.
8. It will be this field (the Centre Reference Number) that we use to link these two tables together.
9. Click on the Edit Relationships button.
10. Click on Create New.
11. Select the first table you want to use from the Left Table Name drop-down menu.
12. Select the field you are linking with from the Left Column Name drop-down menu.
13. Repeat steps 11 and 12 for the linking tables from the Right Table Name and Right Column Name and click OK.
14. Click the Enforce Referential Integrity button (if appropriate) and click on Create.

Once your relationships are in place, you can use the tables to create forms and searches based on all the tables that are related.

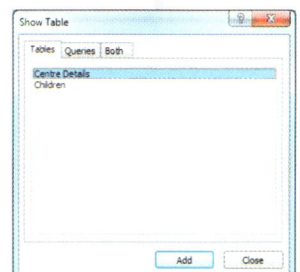

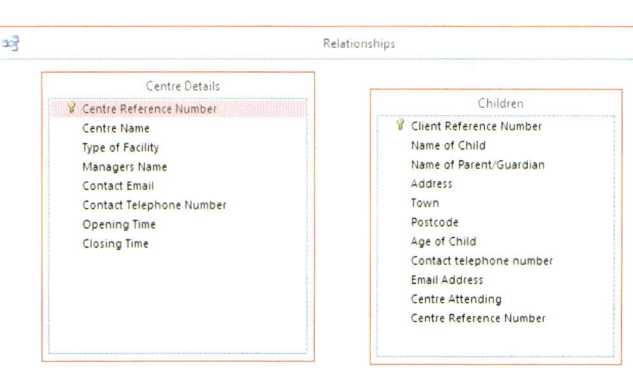

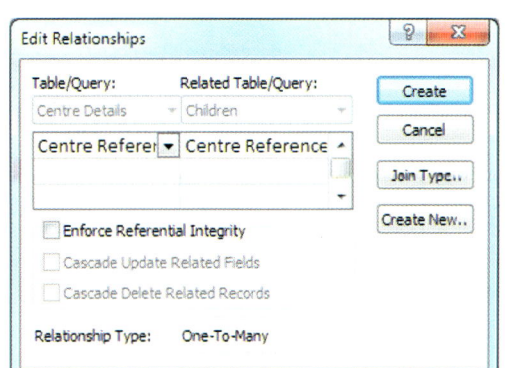

SEARCHING, SORTING AND CREATING REPORTS

Symbol/ term used	Description of use
No Symbol	When you type in text, a number or other without any symbol preceding or following it, the software will match to that word, number or other exactly.
OR	Use OR when you have two or more criteria to match and you would like the software to match on either option.
IN	Use IN if you have more than one criterion in a list – for example, Glasgow, Dumfries and Largs. By entering IN and the criteria in brackets, you can search for multiple criteria.
NOT	If you want to exclude a particular item from your list, use NOT in the criteria field.
NOT IN	If you want to exclude more than one criterion from your list, use NOT IN in the criteria field. Remember that your criteria need to be inserted into brackets for this particular option.

Symbol/ term used	Description of use
<	Less than – Use when you want to search through a field for numbers less than your criteria.
>	Greater than – Use when you want to search through a field for numbers greater than your criteria.
<=	Less than or equal to – Use when you want to search for a particular number or number less than your criteria.
>=	Greater than or equal to – Use when you want to search for a particular number or number greater than your criteria.
<>	Not equal to – Use when you want to exclude a particular number from your criteria.
=	Equal to – Use when you want to search for an exact amount.
Between X and Y	Between two numbers – Use if you want to search between two numbers.

SEARCHING THE TABLE

When you are searching for specific information, you might have to use Control Operators.

When your search criteria is **text** based you can use OR, IN and NOT, or NOT IN.

When your search criteria is **number** based, you can use <, >, <>, =, >=, <=, or Between X and Y.

When your search criteria is **date** based, you can use same options as you would use for **number** based criteria.

WILDCARDS

A **wildcard** is a special character that can stand for either a single character or a string of text. Wildcards are useful when you want the query to look for a range of different possible values, and also when you are not certain exactly what you are looking for, but can give the query some clues to work with.

The symbol we use for a wildcard is the asterisk *

C*	Finds all records that begin with C, with no limit on extra characters
*C	Finds all records that end with C, with no limit on extra characters
C	Contains the letter C anywhere within it

BUILDING A SEARCH

When you are using a database table or tables, there will be occasions where you need to search the table(s) for specific information.

In business, databases might consist of thousands of records, and so it would not be easy or practical to simply 'look' for the information. There is a Query function available in Microsoft Access to address this. To search (query) the data in the tables follow the instructions below:

1. Click on the Create ribbon.
2. Click on Query Design.
3. Add the tables you want to use in your search.
4. Select the fields you want to use in your Query.
5. Enter search criteria in the Criteria row – use the guidelines set out in the table above.
6. Click on the Run button to see if your query has produced the correct results.
7. You can move between the screens by clicking on the View options.

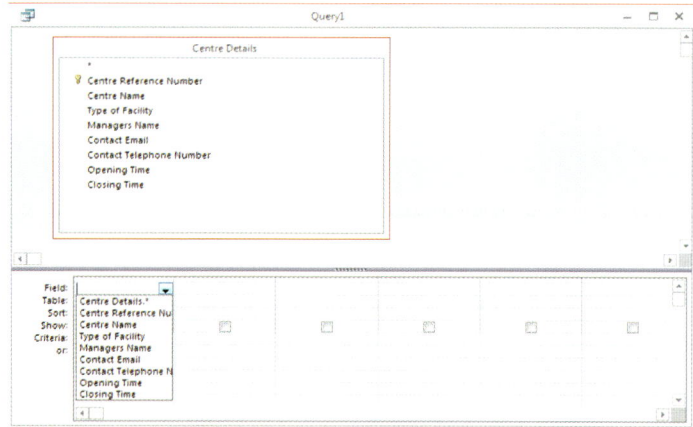

SORTING THE DATA

There will also be a requirement to Sort the data into a specific order, based on up to two fields. To sort the information in your table or your query, follow the instructions below:

1. Ensure that you use the Home ribbon.
2. Click on the Advanced Filter Options button and choose Advanced Filter/Sort.
3. A similar grid to the Query grid will appear.
4. Choose the field or fields that you want to sort your data on.
5. Choose whether you want to sort them in Ascending or Descending order.
6. Then Click on the Filter icon on the toolbar – Apply Filter.
7. You should now see your original data presented in the order you requested.

CREATING A REPORT

The Report tool is used to present the data in tables and queries in a professional way. To create a report based on a table or a query, follow the instructions below:

1. Click on the Create ribbon.
2. Click on Report Wizard.
3. Select the table or query you want to use as the basis of your report.
4. Select the fields you want to appear in your report. Click Next>.
5. If you are asked to group your report based on a particular field, you can select that at this stage.
6. Click Next>.
7. The next stage allows you to sort the data. Click Next>.
8. The next stage allows you to change the appearance of the report.
9. In this last stage, you can enter a Report Title – it's important to choose something meaningful here as it does appear at the top of your report.
10. Click Finish – your report will open automatically.

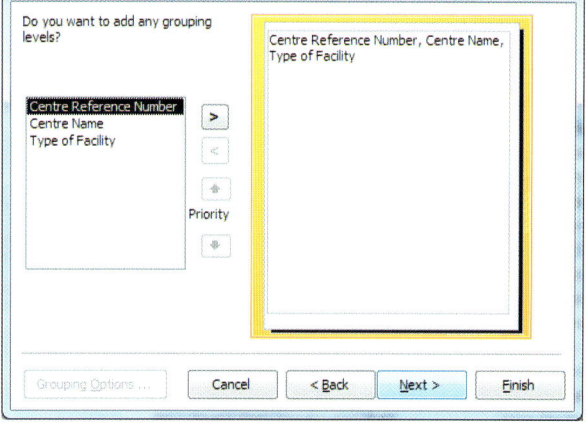

INSERTING HEADERS AND FOOTERS IN YOUR REPORT

As with forms, you need to change to Design View to add a header or footer.

Page Footer – this will appear at the bottom of each page of your report.

Report Footer – this will appear at the end of the data at the end of the report.

For example, in a three-page report the Page Footer would appear the bottom of each of the three pages, whereas the Report Footer would only appear on the last page below the last record displayed.

 VIDEO LINK

To learn more about Reports in Microsoft Access watch the short clip at www.brightredbooks.net/N5AdminIT

 THINGS TO DO AND THINK ABOUT

Look at the report below. What formatting steps would you take to enhance it?

 DON'T FORGET

Use the Create ribbon to create Forms, Queries and Reports.

Centre Details1

Type of Facility	Managers Name	Opening Time	Closing Time
Creche	Suzanne Martin	08:00	18:00
Creche	Angela Levie	07:30	17:30
Nursery	Simon Wilson	08:00	19:00
Nursery	Claire Browne	08:00	18:00
Both	Lesley-Ann Harrower	07:00	20:00
Nursery	Gillian McCombe	07:30	18:00
Creche	Andrew Upton	08:00	18:00
Nursery	Diana Paterson	08:00	19:00
Both	Lucy Mackle	07:00	18:30
Nursery	Amy Sives	07:30	18:30
Both	Rebecca Andrews	08:00	18:30
Nursery	Pauline Harlow	08:00	19:00
Both	June Peebles	07:00	17:30

 ONLINE TEST

Want to test yourself on this topic? Head to www.brightredbooks.net/N5AdminIT

MAIL MERGING, PRINTING AND KNOWLEDGE CHECK: USING A RELATIONAL DATABASE

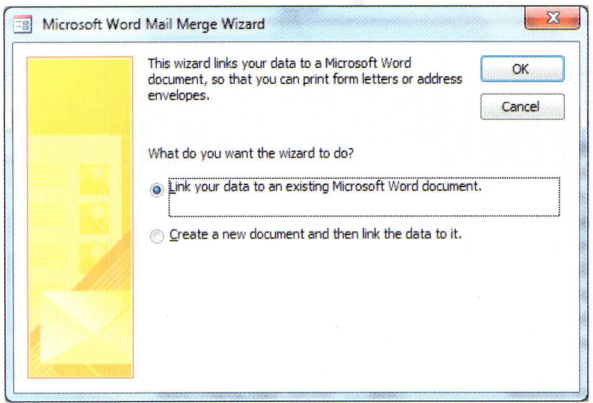

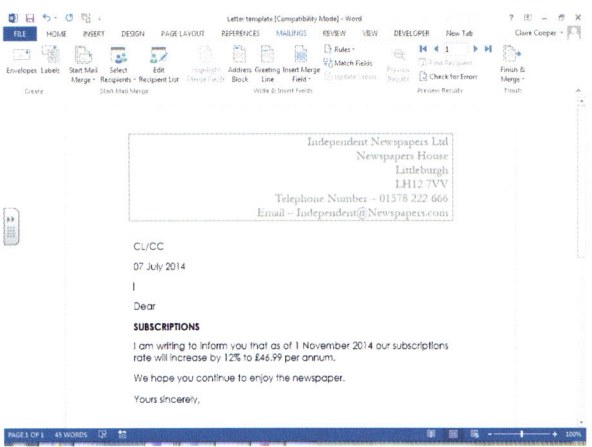

MAIL MERGING

In business, it is normal practice to send out the same letter to many different people. For example, your school might send out a standard letter about a Parents' Information Evening where the content of the letter is the same, but the address details are different.

Mail Merging is a function that we use to link information in a database table or query to a word processed document.

To merge data from a database table or query to a word document, follow the instructions below:

1 Click on the External Data ribbon and click on Mail Merge.
2 From the window that opens, choose from the two options presented:
   - Link your data to an existing Microsoft Word document: use this option if you have already created your document.
   - Create a new document and then link the data to it: use this option if you have not already created your document.
3 Microsoft Word will then open and you will have the option to input the fields from the database table or query you have used.
4 You are now going to use the Mailings ribbon in MS Word:
5 Click on the Insert Merge Field button, and you will see a drop down menu with the Fields present from the Database table or query you used.
6 Use these fields to enter the data you want to merge.
7 When you have done this, click on Finish and Merge to produce your finished document.

PRINTING

PRINTING A TABLE OR A QUERY

To print a table or a query, follow the instructions below:

1 Click on External Data

2 Click on More (in the Export section)

3 Choose Microsoft Word

4 Put a tick in the **Open the destination file after the export operation is complete** box.

5 Click OK.

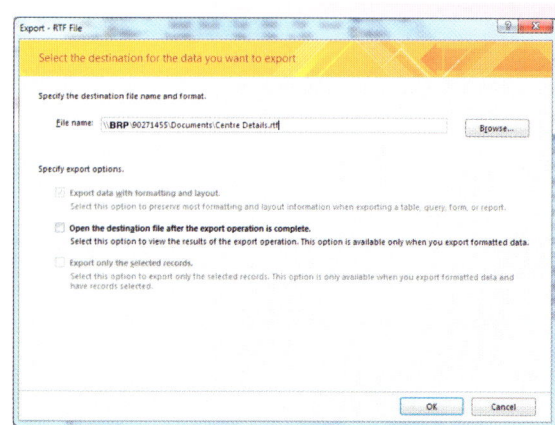

6 The document will now open in Microsoft Word and you can format this as you would any other word document.

PRINTING A FORM OR A REPORT

You can print these directly from Access software. Just remember to make sure that all the data you want to print is visible, and that you have added your name in any appropriate place.

contd

If you want to print an individual form (rather than a list of all the forms) follow the instructions below:

1 Ensure that you are viewing the form you want to print.
2 Click on File.
3 Click on Print.
4 Select the Selected Record(s) option.
5 Click OK.

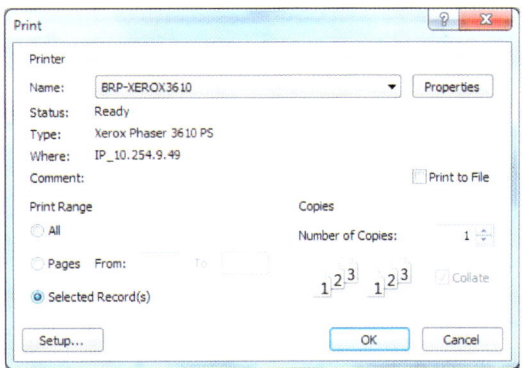

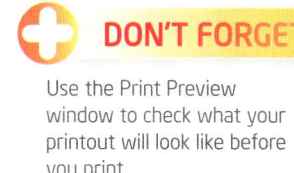

DON'T FORGET

Use the Print Preview window to check what your printout will look like before you print.

KNOWLEDGE CHECK: USING A RELATIONAL DATABASE

HOW DO I MEET THIS OUTCOME?

For Outcome 2 of this Unit, you are required to:

2 Use advanced functions of a relational database to interpret a given brief by:
   2.1 Populating a database, using forms
   2.2 Editing a database
   2.3 Manipulating information in a simple relational database
   2.4 Presenting information in a report, to a professional standard

Use the checklists and tasks below to evaluate your learning from this outcome:

OUTCOME 2: SKILL SCAN

		Green light	Amber light	Red light
2	I can locate and open an existing database file.			
	I can open a table and edit the: • field names • field formatting • records by changing the data, adding new records and deleting records.			
	I can add new fields to a table and format them appropriately.			
	I can create a form and use the form to enter information into a table.			
	I can outline the main features of a relational database.			
	I can create a search using the Query tool to search for records from across different related tables.			
	I can sort the database table or search on two fields.			
	I can produce a database report to a professional standard: • using data from more than one table within the database • inserting a suitable and relevant heading • ensuring that all data are visible.			
	I can merge data from a source in the database to a word document.			
	I can use Page and Report Headers and Footers to show meaningful information.			
	I can print: • a table and a query using the Export to Word function • one selected record in Form view • all records in form view • a Report • Merged Fields in a word processed document.			

ONLINE TEST

Head to www. brightredbooks.net/ N5AdminIT and take the test on this topic.

USING WORD PROCESSING SOFTWARE

USING THE SOFTWARE 1

OUTCOME 3: AN OVERVIEW

For Outcome 3 of this Unit, you are required to:

1 Use advanced functions of word processing to interpret a given brief by:
- 3.1 Editing business documents, applying the house style
- 3.2 Creating and/or editing a table
- 3.3 Importing data from a spreadsheet and/or database dynamically into a business document
- 3.4 Merging appropriate data from a spreadsheet or database into a business document

SOFTWARE AND LAYOUT

For N5 Administration and IT, you need to be familiar with both word processing software and the layout of particular business documents. In this chapter, we will cover how to use the software and go over the layout of some of the documents you might be asked to create in class or for the exam.

Word processing is one of the most frequently used software applications in the business world. It is vital that good administrators have full use of all the available facilities to create and edit documents such as letters, reports, forms, minutes, agendas and itineraries.

All word-processors have a toolbar at the top. This enables you to create a new, blank document, add text and edit it.

FONTS AND SIZES

You must be able to alter the font and font size of text. These are usually available on the toolbar.

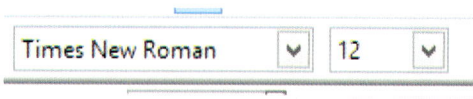

To change the font within a document, highlight the text that you want to alter and then choose your font and size.

A range of different fonts and sizes are available to choose from.

MARGINS

Margins can either be altered by changing the size of the margins in the page layout menu, or by moving the rulers at the top and sides of the document.

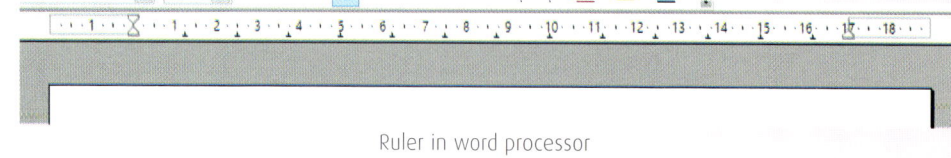

Ruler in word processor

Page layout menu

INSERTING AND DELETING TEXT

You can insert text by clicking with your mouse at any point in the document, and then just typing the new text in. You can delete text either by highlighting the text you want to remove and pressing 'backspace', or by pressing 'delete' on your keyboard.

By highlighting the text with your mouse, you can use the cut, copy and paste options from the Edit menu to move text around the document.

ONLINE TEST

How well have you learned this topic? Take the test at www.brightredbooks.net/N5AdminIT

MANUSCRIPT CORRECTIONS

All documents should be checked before they are sent out. Most companies use a standard set of correction marks to show what editing is required.

In the tasks on the Digital Zone, you will be asked to edit two different types of text:
- text that has been typed up (keyed in) already
- handwritten text.

Sometimes handwriting is difficult to read – but that is part of the challenge!

You will also need to recognise and use **manuscript correction symbols**. These indicate the changes that need to be made to the text you are keying in:

DON'T FORGET

Make yourself familiar with the manuscript correction symbols for the assessments and final assignment.

Symbol/sign	Meaning	Action
the	Delete	Do not type any words that have a line through them.
⅄ a	Insert	Insert the word/s written beside the symbol - ⅄
⅄ #	Insert space	Insert a space in the text indicated by the symbol.
⌒	Close up	Delete space/s in the text.
NP [	New paragraph	Start a new paragraph, where indicated in the text.
⌒	Run on	Join the paragraphs together.
trs ⌷⌷	Transpose	Move the letter/s or word/s as indicated with the underlines.
Stet	Let it stand	Type the word/s with the broken line underneath – ignore the other alterations.
UC or CAPS	Upper case	Change the letter/s or word/s indicated in the text to capital letters.
LC	Lower case	Change the letter/s indicated in the text to small letters.
Bold/italics/underline		Where this is indicated in the margin, an area of the text will be underlined – only format the underlined section.

An example of how this might be displayed in a task is shown below:

The manuscript correction symbols here tell us to make the following changes:
1. LC – change the capital B in Bedding to a lower case 'b'.
2. Trs – change the order of the words underlined – so 'dinner and breakfast' becomes 'breakfast and dinner'.

> day
> The 8-night tour starts and ends in the
> pretty lakeside town of Bled in a 3-star hotel,
> while accommodation on the trek is in
> well-furnished huts. Beds in the huts
> LC   are dormitory style and all Bedding is
> Trs   supplied. Local staff provide dinner and breakfast
> each morning and evening and also prepare
> packed lunches for the day's trek. All you need
> to carry are your own personal items. Any items
> not required on the trek can be left at the
> hotel in Bled.

THINGS TO DO AND THINK ABOUT

In the final assignment, there will be tasks that feature manuscript correction symbols. However, you won't be able to refer to this table, so make sure that you are familiar with the symbols beforehand.

USING THE SOFTWARE 2

Bold, *italic* and underline tools

BOLD, UNDERLINE AND ITALIC

Text can be enhanced by using underline, bold or italic tools. Highlight the particular word or phrase and then press the appropriate button on the toolbar.

This will help to emphasise a particularly important point.

Text alignment tool

TEXT ALIGNMENT

Alignment means that the text is in a straight line. Text is normally aligned to the left but you can highlight blocks of text and highlight them to the right, centre or on both sides.

Centre

Number of Students in Business Education Classes		
Administration and IT		34
Business Management		44
Accounting and Finance		25
Economics		31
Total		134

Right

Text before applying justification

Left

Word processing is one of the most used software applications in the business world. It is vital that good administrators have full use of all the available facilities to create and edit documents such as letters, reports, forms, minutes, agendas and itineraries.

Justified

Word processing is one of the most used software applications in the business world. It is vital that good administrators have full use of all the available facilities to create and edit documents such as letters, reports, forms, minutes, agendas and itineraries.

Line spacing tool

LINE SPACING

Sometimes you might want more space between lines of text than normal, for example, so you can write in comments. This is common practice for university essays. You can select the amount of line spacing you require – for example:

- 1 (single)
- 1.5 (one and a half)
- 2 (double)
- or more.

Here are examples of different types of line spacing:

Single Line spacing: 1

Word processing is one of the most used software applications in the business world. It is vital that good administrators have full use of all the available facilities to create and edit documents such as letters, reports, forms, minutes, agendas and itineraries.

Word processing is one of the most used software applications in the business world. It is vital that good administrators have full use of all the available facilities to create and edit documents such as letters, reports, forms, minutes, agendas and itineraries.

One-and-a-half line spacing: 1.5

DON'T FORGET

Be careful not to overdo the number of fonts, sizes and other text enhancements in one document, as this can make the document look cluttered and unprofessional.

Double Line spacing: 2

Word processing is one of the most used software applications in the business world. It is vital that good administrators have full use of all the available facilities to create and edit documents such as letters, reports, forms, minutes, agendas and itineraries.

INSERTING GRAPHICS

You can add graphics to your word processing documents to make them more interesting or meaningful. There are four types of graphic that you can insert into your document:

- graphic file that has been saved on a storage device
- clip art file that comes as part of your word processor
- shape that comes as part of your word processor
- graphic from the internet that you have copied and can just paste into your document

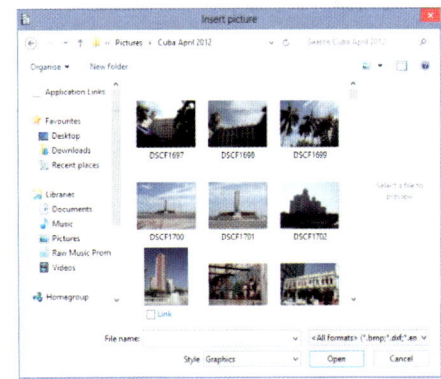

Inserting a graphic

BULLETS AND NUMBERING

EXAMPLE:

Sales Staff	Sales Staff	Sales Staff
1. Smith	• Smith	a. Smith
2. Brown	• Brown	b. Brown
3. Jones	• Jones	c. Jones
4. Edwards	• Edwards	d. Edwards

You can automatically create bullet points or number rows of text by highlighting them and then selecting the appropriate type of formatting from the toolbar.

You will get a greater choice of bullets and styles of numbering if you select bullets and numbering from the Format menu.

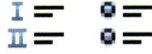

Bullet point/ numbering tool

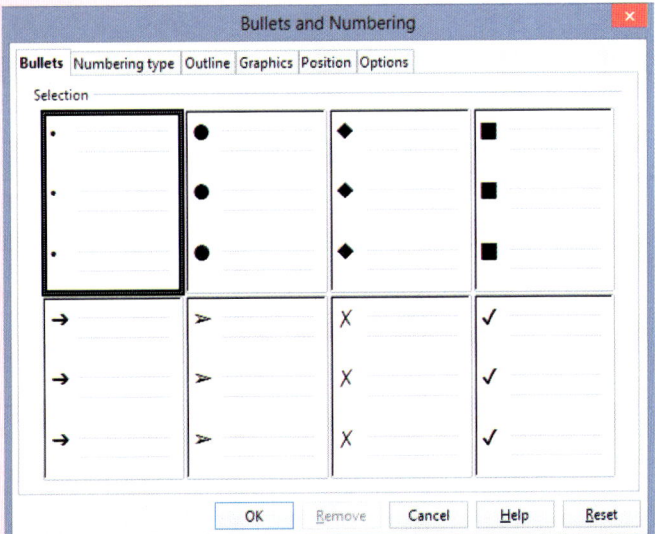

Format menu

 ## THINGS TO DO AND THINK ABOUT

Research the content for a poster about Health and Safety legislation by looking back at the previous Outcome. Create the poster by using word processing software and applying some of the skills you have learned in this Unit.

USING THE SOFTWARE 3

HEADERS AND FOOTERS

These show that a series of pages belong to the same document. They are also very useful if the pages get mixed up or separated. Whatever text you type in, the header or footer option will appear at the top or bottom of every page.

Organising and supporting events – Further useful planning tools and budgeting U1

This book has a header on every page

PAGE NUMBERING

You can automatically number the pages on your document. This is especially important with long documents. There are a variety of styles and numbering you can choose for the page numbering.

BORDERS AND SHADING

You can use borders and shading to highlight areas of text that you want to emphasise.

- Highlight the text that you want to have a border and shade
- Select the border and shading option
- Select the arrangement, style and colour of your border

CREATING AND EDITING TABLES

INSERTING TABLES

Tables can be inserted into any place in your word processing document. Usually the software asks how many rows and columns that you require in your table.

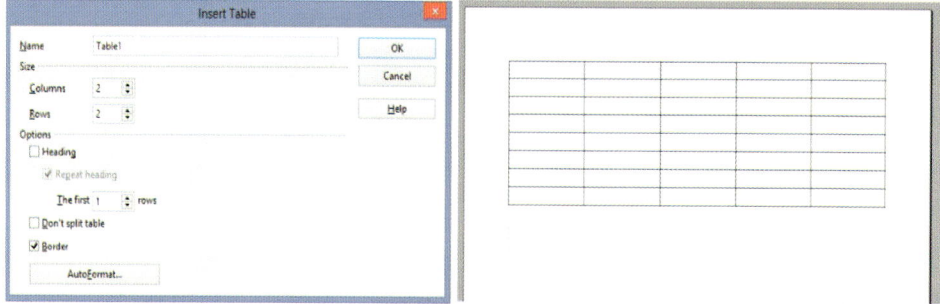

Insert Table menu

ADDING/DELETING ROWS AND COLUMNS

Adding or deleting rows and columns is very simple.

- **Deleting** – click the cursor on a cell in the row or column you would like to delete and then select 'delete row' or 'delete column' from the appropriate menu.

- **Inserting** – click the cursor on a cell in a row or column next to where you would like a new row or column to appear, then select whether you want to insert the column to the left or right or the row above or below.

contd

INSERTING, DELETING AND AMENDING DATA

You can delete, insert or amend data within tables in the same way as any other text.
- **Deleting** data – highlight data, then press backspace or delete.
- **Inserting** data – place the cursor at the correct place and then type.
- **Amending** data – highlight data that you want to change then type the new data.

BORDERS AND SHADING

Highlight the cells that you want to shade and enclose with a border, then select the 'border and shading' option in the same way as you would with an area of text.

MERGE CELLS

Highlight the cells that you would like to become one, and then select 'merge cells'.

ROTATING TEXT WITHIN CELLS

Click on the cell that you want to rotate. Select 'text direction' from the Format menu and then choose the direction you want the text to face.

FORMULAE

You can insert basic formulae into a table in the same way you insert them in spreadsheet software. Once you have inserted the table and you have entered your data, move the cursor to where you want to display your answer. Then:
1 Click on the 'Layout' ribbon of the Table Tools section
2 Click on the 'Formula' option on the toolbar. The window here should appear:

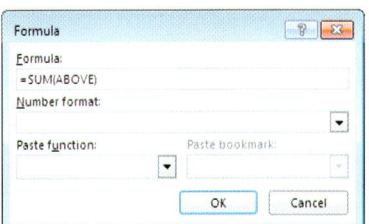

In the following example, we want to **add** the cells together, so we can use 'SUM' in the same way that we do in spreadsheet software – except that in this case, we don't use cell references.

EXAMPLE:

Number of students in Business Education classes	
Administration and IT	34
Business Management	44
Accounting and Finance	25
Economics	31
Total	134

The formula itself will not appear – just the result of the formula.

In this next example, we need to use cell references to perform a **subtraction**.

EXAMPLE:

We have to work out which cell reference is which – the example shown is the same as a spreadsheet, but without the Column Letters and Row Numbers being visible.

Prices			
Item	**Selling Price**	**Cost Price**	**Profit**
Oranges x6	£2.99	£2.08	£0.91

SORTING DATA

Highlight the data that you would like to sort, then select the 'sort' option and click on the column you would like the data to be sorted by.

THINGS TO DO AND THINK ABOUT

Try to recreate your school timetable by creating a table in Word. Use the various functions above to enhance the table – for example, borders, shading, alignment and merging cells.

 **ONLINE**

Follow the link 'How to create a travel itinerary' at www.brightredbooks.net/N5AdminIT to learn more.

DON'T FORGET

Formulae in a table in Word follow the same structure as those in Excel.

 **ONLINE TEST**

Take the test on this topic at www.brightredbooks.net/N5AdminIT

BUSINESS DOCUMENTS: BUSINESS LETTERS

There are a number of different business documents that you could be asked to produce while studying for your N5 Administration and IT course. These include:

- Business letters
- Memoranda
- Reports
- Itineraries
- Meeting documentation – Agenda, Notice of Meeting and Minutes

In this section, we will go through each of these documents and explain why and how they are used by administrators.

HOUSE STYLE

A 'house style' is a standard layout that an organisation uses in all of its documentation to ensure that everything it sends out to customers looks consistent, professional and instantly recognisable.

Businesses usually provide a set of templates for employees to use when they produce documents in the workplace.

The **House style** we use in this book will be:

Font Style	Century Gothic	Font Size	12
Margins	2cm	**Bullet Points**	●
Date Format	13 June 2014	[Insert>Date/time>3rd option]	

TEMPLATES

Organisations usually have templates for business documents. These are documents that have been prepared in advance, and that often contain key information about the business.

Templates have the following advantages – they:

- save time – the template can be used by multiple users at the same time
- create consistency – customers and interested parties receive exactly the same information in exactly the same way each time they receive a communication from the organisation
- look professional – customers and stakeholders will therefore begin to recognise the organisation from its business documents and consistent layout.

BUSINESS LETTERS

A business letter is a formal communication between the organisation and another interested party – for example, customers, shareholders, suppliers and employees. The template used for a business letter is called a letterhead.

Cooper Employment Agency
55A St Anne's Square
WESTEROSS
WR5 9FG

01133 456 764
CEAEnquiries@CEA.org.uk

contd

LETTERHEAD

A letterhead can be presented in many different ways but it should always contain the following information:

- Name of the organisation
- Address of the organisation
- Contact details – telephone number, fax number and e-mail address
- Logo or graphic representing the organisation

A letterhead should always be used when preparing a business letter because the person receiving it will see instantly who has sent it, and will also have the contact information if they need to reply.

KEY TERMS

Reference – This is keyed in below the letterhead and is made up of two sets of initials – the initials of the person who will sign the letter and of the person who keyed the letter.

Date – You should always put the date on the letter and key this in, in full.

Name and address – You might not always have this information, but when you do, you should key this into the space indicated.

Opening – This refers to how we 'open' our letter:

- Dear Sir/madam
- Dear Parent/guardian
- Dear Ms Smith
- Dear Susan

How you open your letter will indicate how formal your letter is and will influence which 'closing' you will use.

Subject line – This is a short description of the purpose of the letter, and should be placed between the opening and the first paragraph.

Closing – There are two options to use when 'closing' your business letter:

- Yours faithfully
- Yours sincerely

If you have not made reference to a name in the opening – for example, Dear Sir/madam – then your closing should be 'Yours faithfully'. If you have made reference to a name in the opening – for example, Dear Ms Smith – then your closing should be 'Yours sincerely'.

Business letters are also always aligned to the left hand side from the reference down to the closing. Formatting can be used on the letterhead and on elements of the letter, but should not be applied to the whole document.

Letters can also extend onto more than one page. If your letter does, then you must ensure that you label the second page appropriately so that both pages can be matched back together if they happened to be separated.

EXAMPLE:

Business letters have a specific layout that should be followed at all times. Here is an example:

> Cooper Employment Agency
> 55A St Anne's Square
> WESTEROSS
> WR5 9FG
>
> 01133 456 764
> CEAEnquiries@CEA.org.uk

Reference ← CC/DF

Date → 13 August 20XX

Name and Address ← Miss Abigail Ross
23 Smith Lane
WESTEROSS
WR6 3RR

Opening ← Dear Miss Ross

Subject → INTERVIEW ARRANGEMENTS

Subject Line → Further to our telephone conversation, I am now confirming the arrangements for your interview on Friday.

Position interviewed for: Personal Assistant to Marketing Director
Date and time: Friday 15th August at 10am

As discussed, please bring proof of identity and your exam certificates with you. As you are scheduled to complete a short attainment test before the interview, we would advise that you arrive at our office at 9.15am. You can find sample attainment tests on our website should you wish to try some practice tests in preparation for the test on Friday.

If you have any further questions relating to the interview or the arrangements, please do not hesitate to contact me.

Closing → Yours sincerely

Signature Space ← (Approximately six line spaces)

Denyse Ferguson
Recruitment Consultant
D.Ferguson@CEA.org.uk

DON'T FORGET

The 8th of September 2014 if keyed in short date format would appear as 8/9/14 – to those recipients used to using American formats this would not read as 8th of September but rather 9th of August.

ONLINE TEST

Test yourself on 'Business documents: business letters' at www.brightredbooks.net/N5AdminIT

> 2
> 13 August 20XX
> Miss Abigail Ross

This is how your second page should begin:

1. The page number
2. The same date as was entered on the first page
3. The name of the recipient.

THINGS TO DO AND THINK ABOUT

1. Try creating a letterhead for your family, using your name and home address. Alternatively, find out what your school letterhead looks like and try to recreate it.
2. Using your letterhead, type up a letter.

BUSINESS DOCUMENTS: MEMORANDA, BUSINESS REPORTS AND ITINERARIES

MEMORANDA

Memoranda or memos are word-processed documents that are used to communicate information internally between different departments or between management and staff.

Memos are useful as they can be sent to more than one person at a time.

TEMPLATE FOR A MEMORANDUM

MEMORANDUM

TO:

FROM:

DATE:

SUBJECT:

IMPORTANT POINTS FOR PREPARING A MEMORANDUM

1 This is an internal business document, so no addresses are required and the document does not require a signature.
2 Formal language is, however, still required.

MEMORANDUM

TO: All sales staff
FROM: Human Resources Manager
DATE: 13 August 20XX
SUBJECT: Performance reviews

All sales staff are reminded that performance reviews will take place week beginning 30 August 20XX. Please ensure that you have completed your performance review documentation beforehand, so discussions between managers and staff can be as productive as possible in the time allocated.

If you are unable to attend at the time scheduled for you, please ensure that you inform your manager and HR consultant.

If performance reviews do not take place as scheduled, this can delay performance-related pay awards being made for September's salary payments.

DON'T FORGET

It's one memorandum (memo) and two or more memoranda (memos)

BUSINESS REPORTS

Business reports are internal business documents that communicate the findings of an investigation or research project to those interested in the results. As with the other documents, there is a template online that you can use for guidance. There is, however, flexibility in how this document is formatted. For example, there is no requirement for the text to be formatted to the left (as in the business letter) and the headings can be either shoulder or paragraph style.

TEMPLATE FOR A BUSINESS REPORT

Report on: ⟵ 1. The title/subject of the report should be indicated at the top of the report.

To: ⟵ 2. The audience (the person or people the report is intended for) should also be indicated at the top.

Date: ⟵ 3. The date indicates to the audience when the report was published.

Terms of reference	
Procedure	
Findings	
Conclusions	
Recommendations	

IMPORTANT POINTS FOR PREPARING A BUSINESS REPORT

1 The section headings are very important, and should be presented in the correct order, and labelled (see template).
2 Formal language should be used in this document – no slang, or shortened abbreviations should be used unless these are required within the context of the report.
3 A signature and address are not required because this is an internal document.

EXAMPLE: BUSINESS REPORT

Report on flexible working opportunities within TBS plc
To: Board of Directors
Date: August 20XX

Terms of reference	Joanne Smith, HR Director, has commissioned this report to investigate what the current flexible working opportunities are and what they could offer in the future. The finished report was due to be submitted by 2 August 20XX.
Procedure	A representative selection of employees (25 per cent) were interviewed by HR staff between 4 January and 17 February 20XX. The discussions focused on the following points: 1. The employees' current working practice. 2. Their impressions of this working practice. 3. Their understanding of the various alternatives.
Findings	1. 76 per cent of employees have a permanent contract and work between 28 and 35 hours per week. 2. Of this 76 per cent, there are a variety of working practices in place – job share, flexi-working and annualised hours. 3. 17 per cent of employees are currently on a temporary contract and felt that they were not in a position to ask for flexible working. 4. From those interviewed, most employees were happy with the options already available. 5. Homeworking, career breaks and term-time working were very popular amongst employees. 6. Employees felt very strongly that the organisation should not use zero-hour contracts.
Conclusions	1. While the majority of our employees are happy with the practices currently on offer, we are unable to interview past employees about their feelings and why they have left our employment. 2. We have a 17 per cent turnover rate of staff and we need to reduce this. 3. We have 19 per cent absence rate and we need to reduce this. 4. 54 per cent of our staff are females under the age of 45.
Recommendations	1. We should review our current policies and introduce new policies in line with our competition. 2. We should introduce a staff exit questionnaire so as to gauge the feelings of staff who are leaving the employment of TBS plc. 3. We need to carry out further investigations into our absence rate and find a way to reduce this in line with national figures.

ONLINE

Look at the example travel itinerary online at www.brightredbooks.net/N5AdminIT
Use this as the basis for creating your own itinerary in the correct format online.

ONLINE TEST

Test yourself on business documents at www.brightredbooks.net/N5AdminIT

ONLINE

Go online and familiarise yourself with the template documents at www.brightredbooks.net/N5AdminIT

ITINERARIES

An itinerary is a travel document prepared by an administrator – the person who has made the travel and accommodation bookings. The itinerary should detail the journey the person is taking – step by step.

TEMPLATE FOR AN ITINERARY

ITINERARY

TRIP TO:

NAME OF TRAVELLER:

DATE(S) OF TRIP:

TIME   DETAIL

IMPORTANT POINTS FOR PREPARING AN ITINERARY

1 Because the person travelling has not made the bookings, the document has to be as detailed as possible.
2 The 24 hour clock is used throughout.

EXAMPLE: ITINERARY

ITINERARY
TRIP TO: ABERDEEN – TRAINING CONFERENCE
NAME OF TRAVELLER: Darren McPhillips
DATE OF TRAVEL: 14 July 20XX
Remember to retain all travel receipts and tickets if a travel expense claim is to be made.

Time	Details
0540 hours	Taxi from home to Edinburgh Haymarket train station
0600 hours	Train departs Edinburgh for Aberdeen
0825 hours	Train arrives Aberdeen
0832 hours	Taxi from train station to Hilton Hotel
0900 hours	Check in for training session
0930 – 1200 hours	Training Session – Performance Reviews
1200 – 1315 hours	Lunch provided in Hotel restaurant
1315 – 1600 hours	Training Session – Dealing with Disciplinary Issues
1615 hours	Taxi from hotel to train station
1655 hours	Train departs Aberdeen for Edinburgh Haymarket
1945 hours	Train arrives Edinburgh Haymarket
2000 hours	Taxi home

THINGS TO DO AND THINK ABOUT

Create an itinerary for a trip between your school and Alton Towers.

BUSINESS DOCUMENTS: MEETING DOCUMENTATION

There are three types of documents that are used in meetings:

- Notice of Meeting
- Agenda
- Minutes of Meeting

NOTICE OF MEETING AND AGENDA

The notice of meeting is sent out to those entitled to attend to inform them of the purpose of the meeting and when and where it will be held. The agenda is attached to the notice of meeting and provides an outline of what will be discussed at the meeting.

TEMPLATE FOR A NOTICE OF MEETING AND AGENDA

Notice of Meeting

A meeting of the <**Insert name of group**> will be held in the <**insert location of meeting**> on <**insert day and date**> at <**time**>.

AGENDA

1 Apologies for absence
2 Minutes from the previous meeting
3 Matters arising
4 <Any other meeting items to be added here>
5 Any other business
6 Date of next meeting
<Name of Secretary>
Secretary

MINUTES OF MEETING

The minutes of the meeting is a written account of what was discussed at the meeting.

TEMPLATE FOR MINUTES OF MEETING

Minutes of Meeting

A meeting of the <**Insert name of group**> held in the <**insert location of meeting**> on <**insert day and date**> at <**time**>.

PRESENT

<Insert the names of those who have attended the meeting>

AGENDA

1 Apologies for absence
2 Minutes from the previous meeting
3 Matters arising
4 <Any other meeting items to be added here>
5 Any other business
6 Date of next meeting

<Chairperson's signature>

<Date>

<Name of Secretary>

Secretary

contd

EXAMPLE OF A MINUTE OF MEETING

EXAMPLE:

Minute of Meeting

Minutes of the Fundraising Committee held in the Meeting Room on 15 July 20XX at 1pm.

PRESENT
Charles Miller (Chairperson), Eilidh Forrester, Gillian Wilson, Eion Watson, Julie Dickson (Secretary).

AGENDA
Apologies for absence
Apologies were received from Catriona Smith and Robert Wylie.
Minutes of previous meeting
The minutes of the previous meeting were taken as read, agreed and signed by the chairperson.
Matters arising
Staff had requested that the location of the next staff fundraising evening was held in the city centre for the convenience of all attending.
Location of staff fundraising evening
We have received quotations from the Hub, Indigo Yard and Centotre. They can all accommodate us on the date of the 27 August. We need to secure ticket sales in order for this event to go ahead.
Promotion of staff fundraising evening
We have found that numbers attending these events in the past have fallen. We must actively encourage members of our department to attend this event. Especially in light of this year's chosen charity – Cancer Awareness Scotland.
Any other business
No other business presented.
Date of next meeting
It has been agreed that the next meeting would be held on 28 July 20XX at 3pm

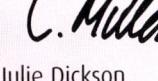

Julie Dickson
Secretary

IMPORTANT POINTS FOR PREPARING MEETING DOCUMENTATION

1 Minutes are prepared after the meeting has taken place and are a formal record of what happened at the meeting and what tasks have to be carried out before the next meeting.

2 There are standard items that always appear:
   - details about who is at the meeting, where they are meeting and when they are meeting
   - who is present
   - who is absent
   - Matters arising
   - Any other business
   - Date of next meeting

3 The secretary prepares the minutes and the chairperson will normally sign them.

 THINGS TO DO AND THINK ABOUT

Create a notice of meeting and agenda for a school charity fundraiser.

 ONLINE

Some examples of these forms can be found at www.brightredbooks.net/N5AdminIT in the word processing section.

ONLINE TEST

Test yourself on 'Business documents: meeting documentation' at www.brightredbooks.net/N5AdminIT

 DON'T FORGET

Your name must be in a footer on all your documents.

OTHER DOCUMENTS AND KNOWLEDGE CHECK: USING WORD PROCESSING SOFTWARE

OTHER DOCUMENTS

You might be asked to create some other documents, including:

- forms
- curriculum vitae
- address labels
- name badges
- certificates

FORMS

A form is a document that is designed to collect information from another person or group of people. It can be designed to be completed by hand or electronically. There are many different forms used in business:

- Application form
- Accident Report form
- Travel and accommodation booking form
- Expenses claim form

CURRICULUM VITAE

A curriculum vitae or CV is a document prepared by an individual who is looking for employment. This document will detail the person's skills, qualities, experience and qualifications.

ADDRESS LABELS

Organisations often use address labels to send out several letters at the same time. Address labels are created by merging the information on a database of addresses into a word document and then printing this onto labels. This is much faster than handwriting each envelope.

Your school probably uses address labels when they send your report cards home!

NAME BADGES

Name badges are created in a similar way to address labels to create labels for people. For example, those attending a conference or training event might be given a name badge to wear for the day.

HOW DO I MEET OUTCOME 3?

For Outcome 3 of this Unit, you are required to:

3 Use advanced functions of word processing to interpret a given brief by:
    3.1 Editing business documents, applying the house style
    3.2 Creating and/or editing a table
    3.3 Importing data from a spreadsheet and/or database dynamically into a business document
    3.4 Merging appropriate data into a spreadsheet or a database into a business document

Use the checklist and tasks on page 67 to evaluate your learning from this Outcome.

OUTCOME 3: SKILL SCAN

		Green light	Amber light	Red light
3	I can format a document by: • selecting and changing font type, size and style • changing margins • recognising and carrying out manuscript corrections • aligning text • inserting line spacing • Inserting graphics • using bullets and numbering • inserting headers and footers • inserting borders and shading • inserting page numbering • inserting, deleting and moving text within a document • applying house style to my documents			
	I can create a table within a word processed document by: • inserting, deleting and amending information • adding or deleting rows and columns • changing the width of a column or the height of a row • merging cells • aligning and positioning text within a cell • applying or removing borders and shading • sorting data within a table • inserting formulae within a table			
	I can recognise and prepare the following business documents: • letterhead • business letter • memorandum • business report • itinerary • Notice of Meeting and Agenda • Minutes of Meeting • forms • curriculum vitae • address labels • name badges • certificates			
	I can print: • finished documents • specific pages from a document			

THINGS TO DO AND THINK ABOUT

Test your knowledge of this Outcome by attempting the tasks below:

⌃ prompt The evening will commence at 7.00 pm ⌃ in the assembly hall with a performance by the
school orchestra. Refreshments will be served afterwards in the gym at 8.30 pm where examples of
NP pupils' work will be on display. ⌈Our guest of honour will be local entrepreneur and former pupil
Mrs Joan Alexander. She has kindly agreed to present the awards and has donated a new award for
UC enterprise to the school.

Yours   *Change Prizegiving to Awards throughout*

J Robertson
Depute Head Teacher   15

1   Name this business document.
2   List the steps you would take to change the margins.
3   Identify each of the manuscript correction symbols shown above and explain what
    you would need to do to the document.
4   What template would be used with this document?

USING TECHNOLOGY TO EXTRACT INFORMATION

USING THE INTERNET TO SEARCH FOR RELEVANT INFORMATION

OUTCOME 1: AN OVERVIEW

For Outcome 1 of this Unit, you are required to:

1 Use technology to extract information and be able to evaluate sources of information by:

   1.1 Searching for and extracting relevant information

   1.2 Outlining key features of reliable sources of information

   1.3 Explaining the consequences of using unreliable internet sources of information

USING THE INTERNET

The internet contains millions of pages of information – a very valuable resource for researching information about a specific topic. Some examples might be:

- searching for train timetables
- finding prices for venues
- downloading maps.

To use the internet properly, you have to understand some key terms:

- Browser
- Website
- Hyperlink
- Search engine
- Web page
- Favourites/bookmarks

INTERNET BROWSERS

You need a browser to access the internet from any device – whether it's a tablet, mobile or desktop. A browser is a software programme that is installed on your device and allows you to access the internet. There are several different browsers available:

- Internet Explorer
- Mozilla Firefox
- Opera
- Google Chrome
- Apple Safari

SEARCH ENGINES

Once you have selected your browser, you need to choose a search engine. The internet contains millions of web pages and sometimes you won't have a specific address. A search engine will help you to find what you need by searching all the web pages available against criteria you have entered, and by filtering the results for you.

The most popular search engine by far is Google. But there are others available:

- Bing
- Yahoo
- Ask.com
- DuckDuckGo

ONLINE

Each browser allows you to access the internet and will have various individual features. To find out more about each browser, use the link at www.brightredbooks.net/N5AdminIT

WEBSITES AND WEB PAGES

A website is a dedicated site on a specific topic or theme. Websites have specific addresses on the internet called URLs – uniform resource locators.

Websites are made up of web pages that also all have their own unique URLs. Most well-designed sites will have a home page and will link to other pages in the site using hyperlinks.

HYPERLINKS

Hyperlinks are used to move quickly between different pages on a website or around the internet in general.

Hyperlinks can also be used in business documents such as e-mails and presentations to take the user directly to a location online.

FAVOURITES AND BOOKMARKS

Favourites and Bookmarks are essentially the same thing – they are browser functions that allow you to save a link to a web page that you access regularly, or would like to access again in the future.

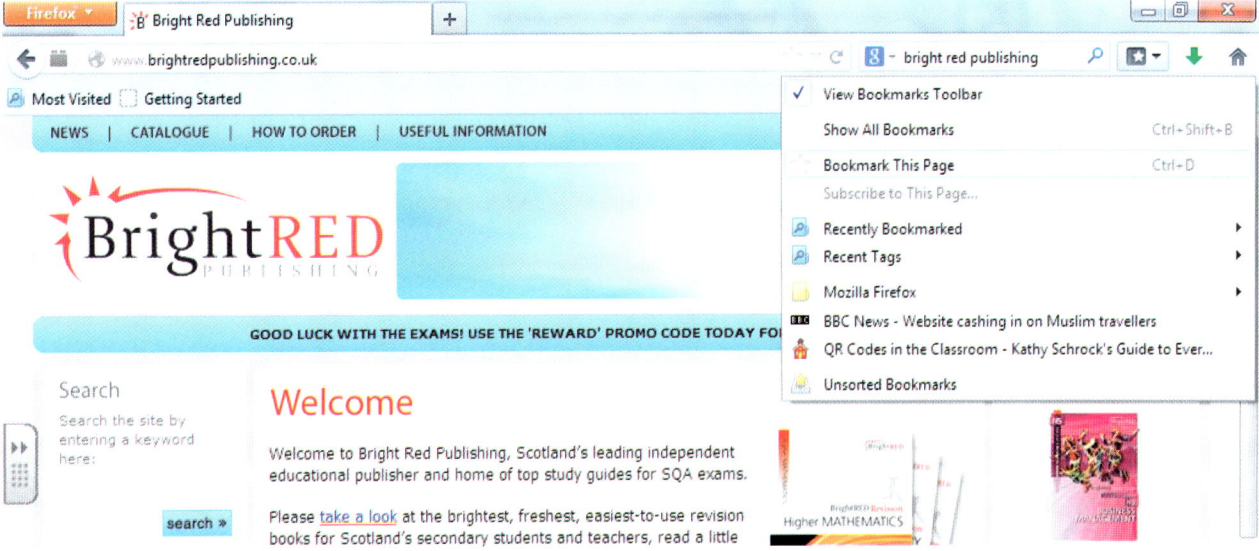

 ## THINGS TO DO AND THINK ABOUT

Use your internet browser to navigate to a website you use regularly and add this site to your favourites. The next time you want to visit the site, use the quick link you've saved in your favourites.

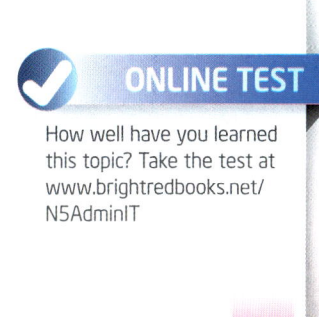

RELIABLE/UNRELIABLE SOURCES OF INFORMATION

KEY FEATURES OF RELIABLE SOURCES OF INFORMATION

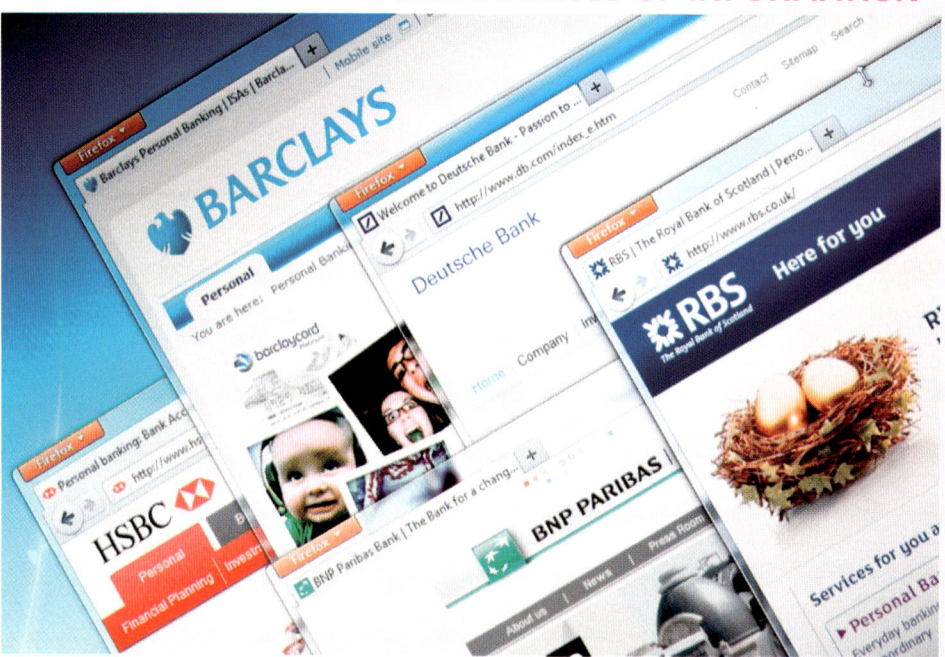

It is important to remember that the internet is a secondary source of information, so if you're at all unsure about a website, check its suitability by asking the following questions:

1 Does this website belong to a well-known business?

2 Is this a reputable organisation?

3 When was this website last updated?

4 Is this a 'secure' website?

 **ACTIVITY** COMPARE THE TWO WEBSITES BELOW AND DECIDE WHICH IS THE MORE RELIABLE:

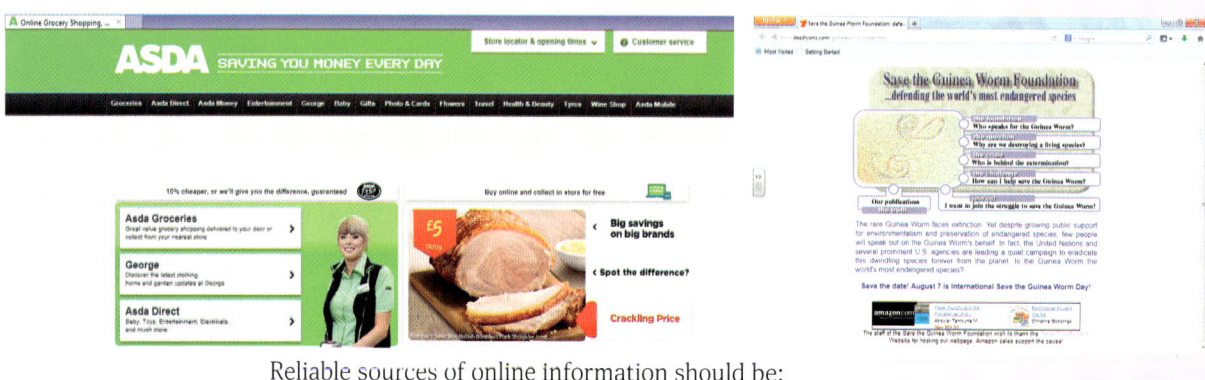

Reliable sources of online information should be:

- up-to-date
- concise
- free from bias
- easily accessible

CONSEQUENCES OF USING UNRELIABLE INFORMATION

It's important to evaluate the information you find online carefully, because it could be:

- false
- out-of-date
- fraudulent
- inaccurate
- biased

If an administrator uses unreliable information, this could have the following negative consequences for the organisation:

- Unreliable information could lead to poor decisions being made – for example, an administrator could research the cost of airfares for a business trip and later find the information was not accurate.

- The organisation could suffer from a loss of reputation as a result of providing wrong or inaccurate information to their customers. This might also result in customers not returning to the organisation and going to a competitor.

- Using out-of-date information could have implications for the organisation – for example, using out-of-date travel information could inconvenience staff, who might miss a train or a bus and be late for an important event.

IDENTIFYING UNRELIABLE WEBSITES

The following features will help you to identify if a website is unreliable.

ADDRESS

Check that the website address ends with one of the recognised suffixes, such as:

.co.uk .com .gov .org .net

If it has a suffix that you don't recognise, approach with caution – it's probably unreliable!

PAGE LAYOUT

Poor page layout, poor-quality graphics and grammar and spelling mistakes usually indicate a poor-quality, unreliable website.

HYPERLINKS THAT AREN'T WORKING

Hyperlinks that don't take you where you expect to go, or that are 'broken' rarely happen on a reliable website.

SITE UPDATES

If the site is being maintained, this will be apparent from the date it was last updated.

SECURITY

Most financial sites or sites where you are asked to enter personal data will have additional security: the URL will begin with 'https' and there will be a lock symbol near the bottom of the page. If a site does not have these indicators, don't enter any personal data.

ONLINE TEST

How well have you learned this topic? Take the test at www.brightredbooks.net/N5AdminIT

DON'T FORGET

The internet is a great source of information, but you should always be careful to check these criteria before deciding if a website is reliable or unreliable.

THINGS TO DO AND THINK ABOUT

Have a look at some of the websites listed below and evaluate how 'reliable' they are:

- www.tripadvisor.co.uk/
- www.visitscotland.com/
- http://en.wikipedia.org/wiki/Main_Page

KNOWLEDGE CHECK: USING TECHNOLOGY TO EXTRACT INFORMATION

HOW DO I MEET THIS OUTCOME?

For Outcome 1 of this Unit, you are required to:

1. Use technology to extract information and be able to evaluate sources of information by:

   1.1 Searching for and extracting/downloading relevant information to interpret a given brief

   1.2 Outlining key features of reliable sources of information

   1.3 Explaining the consequences of using unreliable internet sources of information

Use the checklists and tasks below to evaluate your learning from this Outcome.

SEACHING FOR AND EXTRACTING/DOWNLOADING RELEVANT INFORMATION: SKILL SCAN

		Green light	Amber light	Red light
1.1	I can describe the following terms: • Browser • Search Engine • Website • Hyperlink • Favourites/bookmarks			
	I can identify three different browsers.			
	I can select and use a search engine to find specific information.			
	I can use hyperlinks to navigate my way round a website and use hyperlinks in business documents.			
	I can save sites I use frequently to my favourites/bookmarks.			

 ACTIVITY

Test your knowledge on this area by answering the following questions:

1. Outline the following terms:

   • Browser

   • Hyperlink

   • Bookmark

2. Identify three search engines that can be used to find information online.

3. Identify three hyperlinks displayed on the web page above.

4. The graphic in the margin shows part of the Home Page for the Digital Zone. Describe what is meant by the term Home Page.

OUTLINING KEY FEATURES OF RELIABLE SOURCES OF INFORMATION: SKILL SCAN

		Green light	Amber light	Red light
1.2	I can recognise a website that is 'reputable'.			
	I can list two characteristics of 'reliable' information.			
	I can identify if a website has been updated regularly.			

 **ACTIVITY**

Test your knowledge on this area, by answering the following questions:

1   Why is it important to use reliable information from the internet?

2   Name three characteristics of reliable information.

EXPLAINING THE CONSEQUENCES OF USING UNRELIABLE INTERNET SOURCES OF INFORMATION: SKILL SCAN

		Green light	Amber light	Red light
1.3	I can list three characteristics of unreliable information.			
	I can explain the impact of using unreliable information.			
	I can describe features of websites that can be used to identify unreliable websites.			

 THINGS TO DO AND THINK ABOUT

Test your knowledge of this area by answering the following questions:

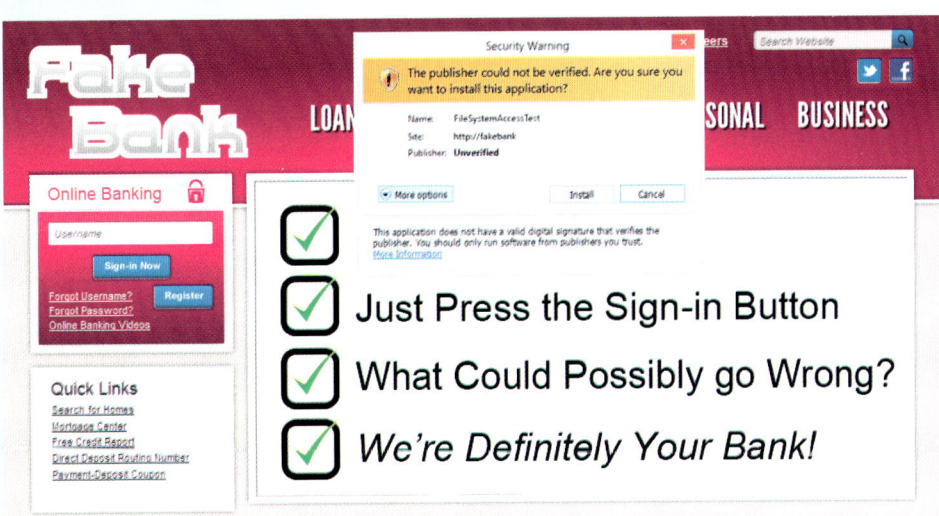

Look at the graphic of the website above. What makes it unreliable?

Describe the possible consequences of using the above website?

USING TECHNOLOGY TO PREPARE AND COMMUNICATE INFORMATION

USING PRESENTATION SOFTWARE

OUTCOME 2: OVERVIEW

For Outcome 2 of this Unit, you are required to:

2   Use advanced functions of technology to prepare and communicate information to a professional standard by:

    2.1   Using functions of multimedia applications to create a presentation

    2.2   Using functions of desktop publishing to produce a document

    2.3   Using electronic methods to communicate information

In this chapter we will look at:

- presentation software
- desktop publishing
- e-mail
- e-diary

USING PRESENTATION SOFTWARE TO PRESENT AND COMMUNICATE INFORMATION

At National 5 level, you are expected to be familiar with presentation software and to be able to carry out the following tasks:

1   Select the appropriate software to create a presentation.

2   Add enhancements such as slide transition, animation and design templates to the presentation.

3   Use slide designs to allow for pictures, text boxes and bulleted lists.

You should be able to move the position of the slides within the presentation and be able to print in various formats:

- Presentation format
- Hand-out format

PRESENTATION SOFTWARE

The most popular presentation software package at the moment is still Microsoft PowerPoint, although others are available:

- Keynote
- Adobe Presenter
- Haiku Deck
- Prezi

Whatever package you decide to use, it must allow you to perform the following functions to complete assignments and exam-based tasks for National 5 Administration and IT:

- Animation
- Action Buttons
- Design Templates
- Slide Transition
- Slide Master options

WHAT DO I ALREADY KNOW?

In this section, we're going to focus on the skills that are unique to PowerPoint, because we've already covered the other skills that are common across the Microsoft suite of software. These are:

- Inserting and deleting text
- Editing existing text
- Formatting text
- Alignment
- Inserting and formatting images and graphics

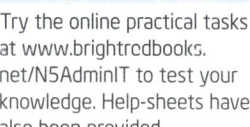

ONLINE

Try the online practical tasks at www.brightredbooks. net/N5AdminIT to test your knowledge. Help-sheets have also been provided.

DON'T FORGET

The online tasks associated with this booklet are all based on Microsoft PowerPoint.

ONLINE

Try the tasks at www. brightredbooks.net/ N5AdminIT to develop your skills in using presentation software.

USING THE FUNCTIONS OF PRESENTATION SOFTWARE

THE RIBBONS

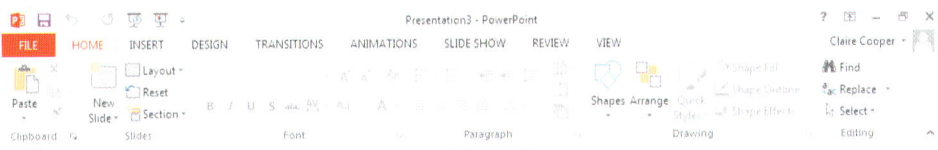

PowerPoint toolbar

Although ribbons have replaced toolbars in Microsoft PowerPoint, many of the icons and shortcuts are the same. All Microsoft software uses the same icons for many of the universal functions. A summary of these common tools can be found in the IT Solutions for Administrators chapter of this book (see page 58).

SLIDE LAYOUTS

There are two slide layouts that are used frequently, because they are very versatile and can be adapted to suit the needs of the user.

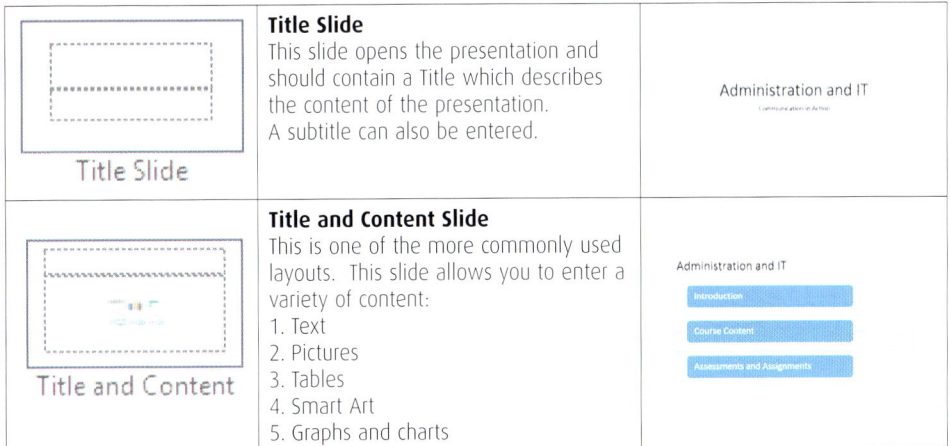

Title Slide	**Title Slide** This slide opens the presentation and should contain a Title which describes the content of the presentation. A subtitle can also be entered.	Administration and IT
Title and Content	**Title and Content Slide** This is one of the more commonly used layouts. This slide allows you to enter a variety of content: 1. Text 2. Pictures 3. Tables 4. Smart Art 5. Graphs and charts	Administration and IT Introduction Course Content Assessments and Assignments

CHANGING THE LAYOUT OF THE SLIDE

If you realise that you have chosen the wrong slide layout, simply click on the Layout button on the Home ribbon:

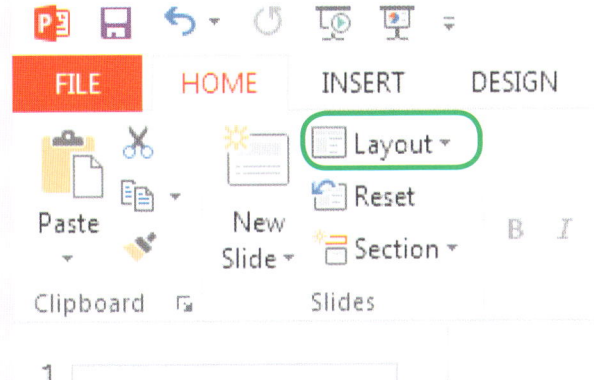

Select your preferred layout.

 THINGS TO DO AND THINK ABOUT

Once you feel confident about the skills you have developed on this spread, have a look at the next few sections and try out the practice exercises there.

 ONLINE TEST

How well have you learned this topic? Take the test at www.brightredbooks.net/N5AdminIT

EDITING SLIDES

ADDING, DELETING AND MOVING SLIDES

ADDING A SLIDE

To add a new slide into your presentation, follow the instructions below:
- Ensure that you are on the Home ribbon.
- Click on Insert Slide.
- You will be presented with a choice of slide layouts.
- Choose the layout best suited to the information you are presenting.

DELETING A SLIDE

To delete a slide from your presentation, follow the instructions below:

1 Using the pane on the left-hand slide of the screen, click on the slide you want to delete.
2 Right click on this slide.
3 From the pop-up menu, choose Delete Slide.

You can also just click on the slide and hit the Delete button on your keyboard.

MOVING SLIDES

To rearrange the order of the slides, follow the instructions below:
1 Using the pane on the left-hand slide of the screen, click and drag the slide to the desired location.
2 You can also use the Cut and Paste options to move slides around.

APPLYING SLIDE DESIGNS AND BACKGROUND COLOUR SCHEMES

ONLINE

Go online to www. brightredbooks.net/ N5Admin11 and open up the Sample Presentation to see how some of these backgrounds might appear.

It's common to enhance the presentation by including a common theme or background colour in the slides.

APPLYING A SLIDE DESIGN

To apply a slide design, follow the instructions below:
1 To choose and select a slide design, click on the Design ribbon

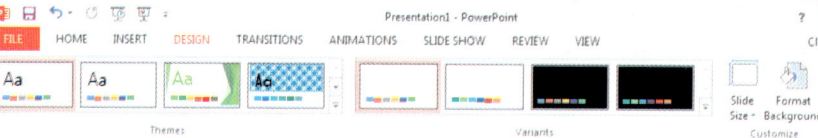

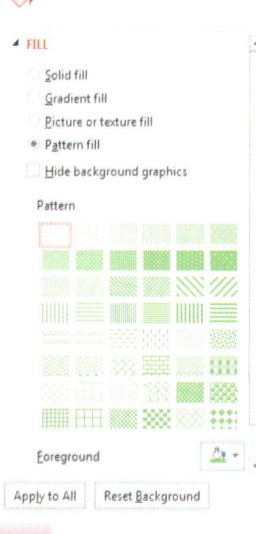

2 The toolbar has two main sections – themes and variants.
   - Themes – this is the main design template
   - Variants – this option displays the variants of the themes. Once you select a theme, the contents of this option will change.

3 Click on the icon of your preferred choice and your presentation will change to reflect the choice you have made.

FORMATTING THE BACKGROUND USING A DESIGN TEMPLATE

When you are using the design templates, you can format the background of each slide by following the instructions below:
1 Click on the Format Background button on the Design ribbon.
2 A number of choices appear. Select how you want to format the background of each slide.
3 When you are happy with your selection, click on the Apply to All button.

FORMATTING THE BACKGROUND WITHOUT A DESIGN TEMPLATE

You can still change the colour of the background of the slide without applying a design template. Simply click on the Format Background button and select your choices.

CREATING CHARTS AND TABLES WITHIN A SLIDE

CREATING TABLES

To create a table in a slide, follow the instructions below:

1. Ensure that you are using the correct slide layout – Title and Content Slide is very useful for this.
2. Click on the icon for a table within the slide layout.
3. Choose the number of columns and rows you want your table to have.
4. If you are using any Word version after 2010, you will see new ribbons appear on screen:

These ribbons now allow you to format the table, format the text in the table, format the borders and shading, and to add further columns and rows or delete elements of the table.

5. Once you are happy with the design of the table template, key in the text you want to display.

CREATING A CHART

Creating a chart in presentation software is similar to creating a chart in spreadsheet software:

1. Ensure that you use an appropriate slide layout to create your chart – any layout with content built in will allow you to do this.
2. Click on the icon for Insert Chart.
3. Select the type of chart you want to use.
4. You will now see a screen like the one below:

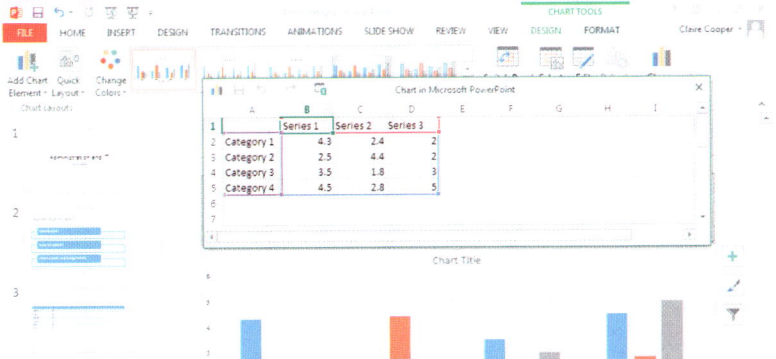

5. The screen should show a pop-up window that should appear to resemble a spreadsheet.
6. Enter your data, as you would do in a spreadsheet.
7. As you edit the data that is pre-set, the chart will change.
8. Once you are satisfied with the changes you have made, close the spreadsheet window to see only the chart.

THINGS TO DO AND THINK ABOUT

Open up an existing presentation and apply some of the techniques you have just learned to enhance the finished product.

DON'T FORGET

If you need to change any data in the chart, simply click on the Edit Data button on the Chart Tools>Design ribbon.

ONLINE TEST

How well have you learned this topic? Take the test at www.brightredbooks.net/N5AdminIT

VIDEO LINK

Head to www.brightredbooks.net/N5AdminIT to watch the tutorial on using presentation software.

IMPORTING DATA AND USING SLIDE MASTER

IMPORTING DATA FROM OTHER PACKAGES

As Microsoft offers a suite of integrated packages (as do most other well-known office-based brands) it is very straightforward to import data from one package into another.

IMPORTING DATA FROM A WORD PROCESSING PACKAGE

You can import data from a word processed document into presentation software by following the instructions below:

1 Ensure that you are on the Home ribbon.

2 Click on New Slide and when the menu appears choose Slide from Outline.

3 The software will then insert slides appropriate to the content in the word document you chose.

IMPORTING DATA FROM A SPREADSHEET

You can integrate both spreadsheet data and charts from spreadsheet software into presentation software by following the instructions below.

(Some people prefer to use a spreadsheet to create a chart, rather than using the built-in chart option in the presentation software.)

1 Insert the slide layout you want to use to view the data.

2 Open up the spreadsheet file you want to use.

3 Highlight and copy the relevant data.

4 Navigate back to the presentation and paste this into the relevant slide.

IMPORTING IMAGES

You can import the following types of image into presentation software:
- photographs you have saved on your computer
- online images from the web
- screenshots
- photo albums

You can insert any of these by following the instructions below:

1 Click on the Insert ribbon.

2 Click on the image option you prefer.

3 Select the file from its location on your computer.

4 Click OK to insert.

You can also insert video and audio into your presentation in a similar way – the menu options for these can also be found on the Insert ribbon.

DON'T FORGET

You can use the same steps to copy a chart from a spreadsheet to a presentation.

USING SLIDE MASTER WITHIN PRESENTATION SOFTWARE

WHAT IS SLIDE MASTER?

You can use the Slide Master option to edit the design and layout of each type of slide available in presentation software.

By using the Slide Master option you can change the:
- design
- background
- colour, styles, size and type of fonts
- type of bulleting used
- positioning of boxes and fields and footer objects within each slide.

contd

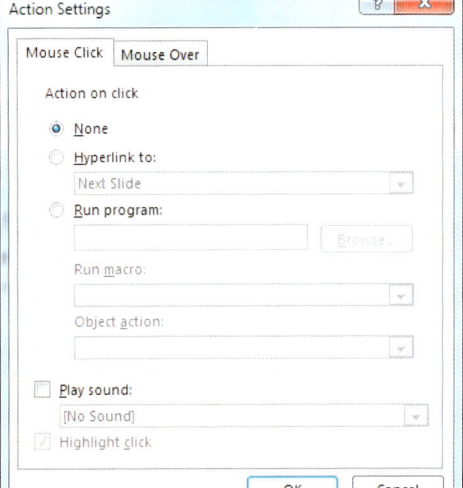

You can save lots of time by using Slide Master to set these changes, because they will then automatically be applied to all the future slides you insert and all the slides that are already in the presentation.

HOW TO USE SLIDE MASTER

Follow the instructions below to open, close and navigate through Slide Master:

To **open** Slide Master:
- click on the View ribbon
- click on Slide Master

To **close** Slide Master:
- close Master View

To **navigate** through Slide Master:
- use the panel on the left-hand side of the screen

ADDING FOOTER OBJECTS IN SLIDE MASTER

You can add footer objects by following the instructions below:
- Open Slide Master from the View ribbon.
- Click on the Insert ribbon.
- Click Header and Footer.

This option allows you to insert:
- date/time
- slide numbers
- footers

You can choose to insert these on each slide or on printed handouts and notes pages.

USING SLIDE MASTER TO INSERT ACTION BUTTONS

You can use Action Buttons to take you quickly to other locations in the presentation.

Locate the Action Buttons options by following the instructions below:
1. Click on Insert.
2. Choose Shapes.
3. At the very bottom of this menu, you will find a section on Action Buttons:

Action Buttons

You can use the first two arrow icons highlighted above to move forwards and backwards through a presentation.

You can also use the other icons highlighted above for a variety of other functions, including:
- Moving straight to the beginning of the presentation
- Moving straight to the end of the presentation
- Home
- Providing Information
- Undo
- Film
- Document
- Sound
- Help
- Custom

4. When you click on any one of these options, click and drag the button to the desired size.

5. Once this is complete a window will open prompting you to choose the end location after the action (clicking on the button must take you somewhere).

THINGS TO DO AND THINK ABOUT

Think about how action buttons could be useful and apply these to a presentation you have used in the past.

DON'T FORGET

The slide layouts you intend to use in your presentation will need to be changed here.

ONLINE TEST

How well have you learned this topic? Take the test at www.brightredbooks.net/N5AdminIT

ONLINE

Develop your understanding of Slide Master by trying some of the online practice tasks at www.brightredbooks.net/N5AdminIT

TRANSITIONS, ANIMATIONS AND PRINTING

TRANSITIONS

The aim of a presentation is to deliver information to a large audience in an engaging way and the slide transition and object animation functions of the software will help you to achieve this.

Slide transition refers to the process of moving between two slides in a presentation.

Slide transition options can give your presentation a more controlled feel, and can also improve the experience for the viewer.

INSERTING TRANSITIONS

You can insert transitions into your presentations by following the instructions below:

1 Click on the Transitions ribbon

2 You are presented with a variety of options on the ribbon.

3 When you have selected an option, the Effect Options button becomes available so you can personalise this option.

4 You can also add sound to your transition.

5 You can also adjust the speed of the transition.

 **ACTIVITY**

Try opening one of your practice presentation tasks and add animation to it to see the impact that each option has.

ANIMATIONS

Presentation software provides users with the facility to animate text, pictures/graphics and other objects in the slides. There is a dedicated ribbon for this function.

There are two options for animations: you can either animate individual objects or apply the same animation scheme to all slides.

ANIMATING INDIVIDUAL OBJECTS

You can animate individual objects by following the instructions below:
1 Highlight the item you want to animate.
2 Click on the Animation ribbon.
3 Choose the Animation option: Entrance, Emphasis or Exit.
4 Click on the Preview button to see how this effect will look in your presentation.

contd

ANIMATING THE ENTIRE PRESENTATION

You can apply animations to the master slide template for the slide layout you have chosen. The animation effects will then automatically be added to all the slides in your presentation and to any additional slides you insert using that layout.

TYPES OF ANIMATION

You can use the following types of animation:

- **Entrance animation** – this animates the text or object as it appears on screen.

- **Emphasis animation** – this animates the text or object of a particular slide to emphasise it.

- **Exit animation** – this animates the text/objects before you move onto the next slide.

PRINTING

When printing your finished presentation you must consider what your printing needs are:

- Do you need to print each slide on a full page?

- Do you intend to provide your audience with a copy of the presentation?

- Do you need to add notes to your copy?

PRINTING YOUR PRESENTATION

To print your presentation, follow the instructions below:

1 Click on File.

2 Choose Print.

In the print window, you can now see a Print Preview of your presentation.

3 In the Settings option, you can choose what you want to print:

- all the slides

- selection of slides

- current slide

- custom range

4 In the Settings option, you can also choose how you want your presentation to look when it's printed:

- full page slides

- handouts – with a choice of how many slides you want to see on each page.

 THINGS TO DO AND THINK ABOUT

You will probably be given specific printing instructions in your assessments and final assignment, so make yourself familiar with this menu and the options available within it.

USING DESKTOP PUBLISHING SOFTWARE 1

DESKTOP PUBLISHING: AN OVERVIEW

Desktop publishing (DTP) has revolutionised the way that newspapers, magazines and brochures are produced. It's now relatively straightforward to place and manipulate text and graphics on your computer to produce print-ready, high-quality materials.

In N5 Administration and IT you will be asked to create a variety of different business documents. While you can create most of these documents using word processing software, there are some that are better suited to desktop publishing software – for example:

- business cards
- menus
- leaflets/booklets
- posters
- certificates

USING TEMPLATES

Most DTP packages come with a large number of templates so you don't have to create one yourself. A template is a document that has been prepared in advance and all you have to do is replace the text and/or graphics with your text and/or graphics.

Here is a small selection of invitation templates:

When you open up the template it is simple to change the text or graphic to suit your needs. This saves a great deal of time and effort and means that you can create a professional-looking document, even if you have no design experience.

Baby Boy Celebration

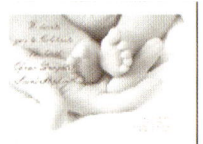
Baby Girl Celebration

Christmas Party

Christmas Tree

Dinner Party 1

Dinner Party 2

Floral Square

Hen Night 1

Hen Night 2

Masquerade Ball

New Years Eve

Wedding 1

Wedding 2

Wedding Day

Wine Tasting Evening

To
Their Name

You are invited to my
DINNER PARTY

from
Sender's Name

00/00/00

TIME 00:00

Address Line 1, Address Line 2, Address Line 3, Address Line 4
Tel: (123) 456 7893, Mobile: (123) 456 7894, Fax: (123) 456 7895
name@home.com

SET AND CHANGE MARGINS

You can change the margins of your page by choosing margins from the Insert menu.

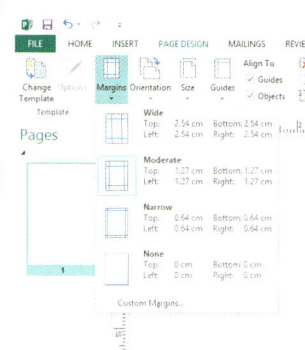

NON-PRINTING GUIDELINES

DTP packages allow you to create non-printing guidelines. These work as follows:
- Click on Guides.
- Drag the rulers onto the page.
- The rulers will leave coloured guidelines that you can use to ensure your text and graphics boxes are aligned.
- When you print the document, the lines don't print out.

INSERT, FORMAT, DELETE AND MOVE TEXT

INSERTING TEXT USING TEXT FILES

One of the great advantages of DTP is that you can use text files that have been created previously using a word processor. To insert text using text files, follow the instructions below:

1 Select Insert File from the Insert menu.
2 Select your word processed file from your documents or portable drive.
3 You can now alter the position of the text box by using the pointer or the handles.

INSERTING TEXT USING TEXT BOXES

To insert text using text boxes, follow the instructions below:

1 Select Draw Text Box from the Insert menu and draw the box in the position you want the text to appear.
2 Choose the font, size, alignment, colour and effects you want from the toolbar.
3 Type your text.

FORMATTING TEXT

To alter the format of text in a text box, follow the instructions below:

1 Highlight the text you want to change.
2 Go into the Home menu.
3 Click on settings you want to change – for example, alignment, bold or underline.

DELETING TEXT

To delete text or a text box, follow the instructions below:

1 If you want to delete a word or line of text, highlight it and press delete.
2 If you want to delete a text box, select the text box and press delete.

MOVING TEXT

To move text or a text box, follow the instructions below:

1 If you want to move a word or line of text, highlight it, cut it, insert the pointer to the appropriate place and paste it.
2 If you want to move a text box, hold the mouse down on the text box, move to the new position and then let go.

DON'T FORGET

Use the pointer tool and the handles to move your text box if you are not happy with its position.

VIDEO LINK

Head to www. brightredbooks.net/ N5AdminIT and check out the tutorial for getting started with Microsoft Publisher.

ONLINE TEST

Test yourself on this topic at www.brightredbooks.net/ N5AdminIT

THINGS TO DO AND THINK ABOUT

Practise using DTP software by creating a business card using Microsoft Publisher.

USING DESKTOP PUBLISHING SOFTWARE 2

INSERTING A GRAPHIC

To insert a graphic into your DTP document, follow the instructions below:

1 Select pictures from the Insert menu:

2 Double click on the graphic you want from within your photos folder or portable drive.

3 Once your graphic is on the page, you can resize it by dragging the handles on the corners.

4 You can then use the pointer to move the graphic to the appropriate place on the page.

5 You can keep resizing and moving the graphic to a new position until the layout looks exactly as you want it.

INSERTING HEADERS AND FOOTERS

It's important to remember that:

- whatever you put in the header will appear at the top of every page in your document
- whatever you put in the footer will appear at the bottom of every page in the document.

TO INSERT A HEADER OR FOOTER

To insert a header or footer, follow the instructions below:

1 Select Header from the Insert menu.

2 A box called Header will appear. Insert and format the text you want here.

3 This will now appear at the top of every page.

4 Footers work in exactly the same way.

VIDEO LINK

Learn more about inserting images by watching the tutorial at www.brightredbooks.net/N5AdminIT

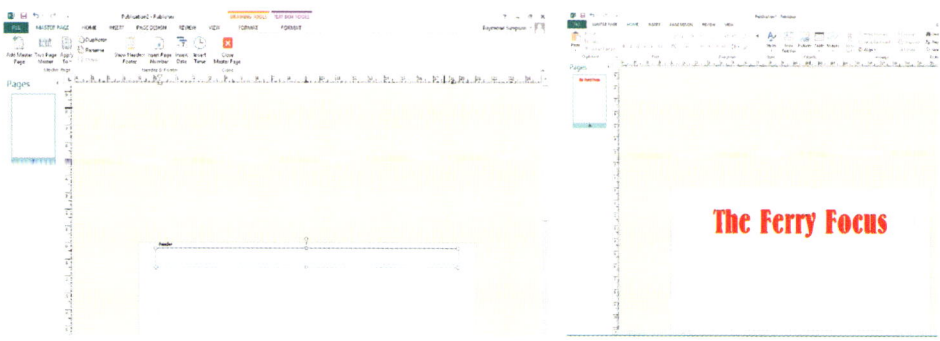

The Ferry Focus

BORDERS AND SHADING

BACKGROUND COLOUR

To alter the background colour, follow the instructions below:

1   Select Background from the page design layout.

2   Select and click on the colour you want.

SHADING

To create shaded colour panels to make your text stand out, follow the instructions below:

1   Select and click on the text box.

2   Right click the mouse.

3   Select the shape fill icon and then choose your colour.

4   You have now shaded your text box.

5   You can also create coloured panels by using the shapes from the Insert menu and changing the fill colour.

BORDERS

To insert borders into your page to make it look more interesting, follow the instructions below:

1   Select Borders & Accents from the Insert menu.

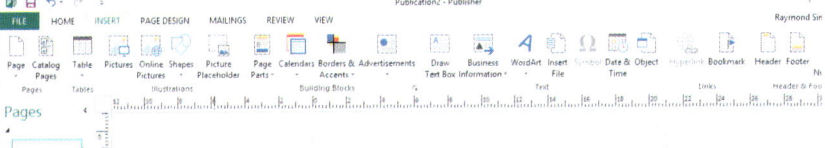

2   Select a border.

3   Use the handles to make it the same size as your page.

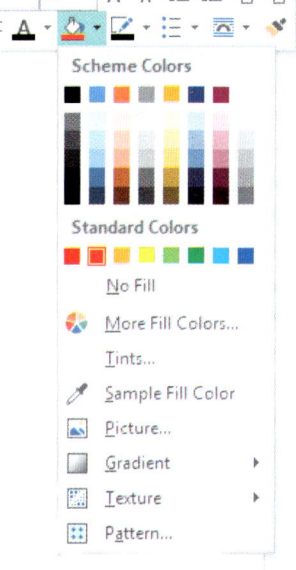

DON'T FORGET

Headers and footers can include automatically changing information such as page numbers.

ONLINE TEST

How well have you learned this topic? Take the test at www.brightredbooks.net/N5AdminIT

THINGS TO DO AND THINK ABOUT

Recreate and improve the school canteen menu using DTP software.

…AIL

USING ELECTRONIC METHODS TO COMMUNICATE INFORMATION

E-mail is the most common way to communicate electronically. It is used by most organisations to communicate formally and informally with employees and customers. E-diaries are used as an organisational tool to plan and prepare for events and other business activities.

WHAT IS E-MAIL?

The Oxford Online Dictionary defines e-mail as:

 Messages distributed by electronic means from one computer user to one or more recipients via a network.

Each user must have an e-mail address and must access their e-mail to receive the message sent to them.

An e-mail address tends to have a standard format: name@business.co.uk

There are various e-mail providers available and most allow access to their system free of charge. They include:

- Microsoft Outlook
- Gmail
- Hotmail
- Yahoo

You have probably been allocated an e-mail account through your educational establishment, which will include your name or username. When you sign up for an e-mail account with an independent provider, you can choose your own username. Think carefully about the username you choose – you might have to use this to contact potential employers in the future.

USING E-MAIL IN THE WORKPLACE

Advantages of e-mail	Disadvantages of e-mail
E-mail is considered to be a relatively quick way to send and receive messages and attachments.	Unless the receiver of the e-mail opens their account regularly, they might not receive the information in a timely fashion.
Messages and attachments can be sent anywhere in the world, as long as both users have e-mail accounts.	SPAM and JUNK e-mails can be frustrating for e-mail users.
The costs associated with e-mail are low – the cost is thought to be less than the cost of sending packages through the post – and it is eco-friendly because it reduces the use of paper.	If you are experiencing technical problems with connecting to the internet, this can make it challenging to access and respond to messages or to send messages.
E-mails can be sent to more than one person at a time (mailing lists/group e-mails).	
Some e-mail systems allow you to create folders to store your e-mails for future reference.	

COMPOSING AND SENDING E-MAIL

To compose an e-mail, you must first access your account and click on New E-mail:

1 Your provider will not normally require you to enter your own e-mail address in the From box, unless you have access to more than one address – then you might be asked to specify which one you want to use.

2 You must enter the e-mail address of the person you want to send your e-mail to. If you have their address saved in your address book, click on 'To:' and your address book will open. Then click on the address and it will appear in the 'To:' box.

contd

3   It is good practice to enter a short description in the Subject Line box. This should outline the topic/theme/intent of your e-mail. This is similar to the Subject Line in a business letter.

4   While an e-mail is classed as an informal method of communication, it should still have an Opening and a Closing:

EXAMPLE:

Openings: Dear All [Names]/Good Morning [Afternoon, Evening]/Greetings
Closings: Regards, With Thanks, Yours

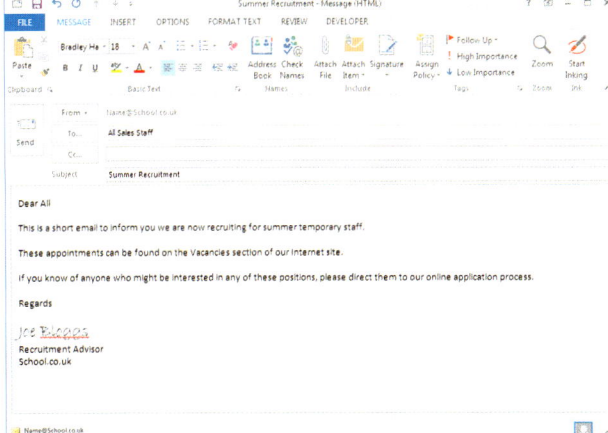

ADDRESS BOOKS

An Address Book allows you to store the e-mail addresses of those people who contact you regularly. This is also known as your Contacts List.

URGENT E-MAILS

! High Importance

You can highlight that an e-mail is urgent by clicking on the 'High Importance' button on the toolbar. This will then appear in their Inbox with a red exclamation mark beside it, so it stands out from the other e-mails.

ADDING ATTACHMENTS

You can add files as attachments to e-mails. To do this, follow the instructions below:
1   Compose your e-mail as normal.
2   When you want to attach a file, click on the paperclip icon with 'Attach File' below.
3   You will then be prompted to locate the file from your own storage area.

Files can take up a lot of space both in your Sent items folder and in the Inbox of the person receiving the e-mail, so always advise before you send an attachment in case it can be shared in another way.

CREATING A SIGNATURE

If you are sending e-mails on a regular basis, you can create a signature for yourself that will automatically appear at the bottom of your e-mails. To do this:

1   Click on Signatures on the Message ribbon.

2   The window shown should appear.

3   Click on New.

4   You will be asked to assign a name to the signature – you could have more than one option for different purposes.

5   You can then create a signature in the bottom panel: at this point the formatting options will be available.

6   Include your Name, Title and Contact details.

DON'T FORGET

It is important to communicate clearly in a professional e-mail. Don't use slang or jargon because it could be misinterpreted in this context.

VIDEO LINK

Watch the tutorial explaining this at www.brightredbooks.net/N5AdminIT

ONLINE TEST

How well have you learned this topic? Take the test at www.brightredbooks.net/N5AdminIT

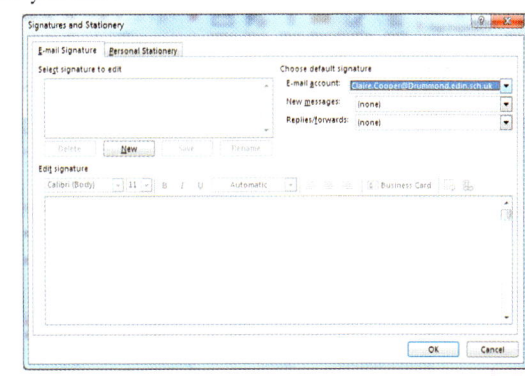

THINGS TO DO AND THINK ABOUT

Head to your e-mail account and create a signature for yourself.

EMERGING TECHNOLOGIES AND E-DIARIES

EMERGING TECHNOLOGIES

Over the past few years, technological advances have revolutionised the way we work and the way we communicate.

The following technologies have had a particular impact:

BLOGS - These are online journals. They are commonly used to record a person's thoughts and feelings on a particular topic or theme.

PODCASTS - These are audio recordings that can be downloaded to your phone or mobile device, so you can listen to them when it's convenient for you.

VODCASTS - These are video recordings that can be downloaded so you can view them when it's convenient for you.

WEBSITES - While websites aren't new, the growth in e-commerce has meant more and more businesses are creating websites so their customers can purchase their products, use their services or communicate with them.

SOCIAL MEDIA - Social media sites are constantly changing and evolving, but are essentially designed to allow people to share their lives with friends, family and business colleagues online – and to make new friends or contacts. Some examples of these are Facebook, Twitter, Instagram and LinkedIn.

VIRTUAL LEARNING ENVIRONMENTS - Virtual Learning Environments (VLEs) require the user to login to a secure area to access resources and tools to support their learning. Your school might use a VLE to provide you with learning opportunities. iTunesU is a very popular VLE, which is available to users with an iPad. Edmodo has also grown in popularity. Schools in Scotland have access to GLOW – the national VLE for education authorities in Scotland.

USING AN E-DIARY

An electronic diary can be a useful tool for administrators. If your organisation is using a system like Microsoft Outlook, users can share their diaries with their assistants, and

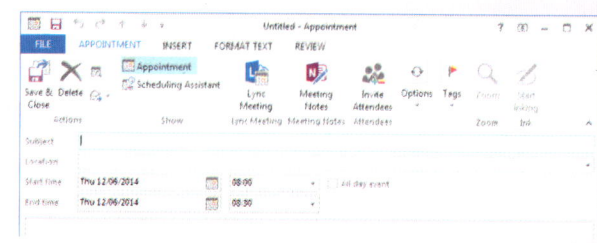

appointments and calendar entries can be entered and amended very easily.

With an e-diary, there is less possibility of double bookings and it also allows you to set reminders, so that you are prompted about a meeting or event you have to attend.

SCHEDULING AN APPOINTMENT

Note that different e-mail providers will use slightly different terms in their calendar function. The following examples and instructions are all based on Microsoft Outlook.

contd

To schedule an appointment, follow the instructions below:
1 Open the Calendar function provided to you by your e-mail provider.
2 Click on New Appointment.
3 Enter the topic/subject for the meeting.
4 Enter the Location.
5 Enter the start and end dates and times.
6 Type in any messages about the meeting/event into the main panel.
7 To invite others to the meeting, click on Invite Attendees.
8 Enter the e-mail address of those people you want to attend with you.
9 When you are finished, click on Save and Close. Your meeting will then be saved in your calendar on the date you entered.

SETTING A REMINDER AND SCHEDULING RECURRENT MEETINGS

To set a reminder and schedule recurrent meetings, follow the instructions below:
1 Open up the meeting you have scheduled.
2 Click on the Options button on the ribbon and choose Reminder.
3 You will be given the option of how long before the event you want to be reminded.
4 In this same Option button, you can choose to schedule recurrent meetings by clicking on Appointment Recurrence.
5 You can then specify how often and when the meetings will be taking place.

ACCESSING OTHER USERS' CALENDARS

To share your calendar with other users, follow the instructions below:
1 Click on the Folder ribbon.
2 Click on Share Calendar.
3 Enter the name or names of those people you want to share the calendar with.
4 You can select how much access they have with the other options in this window.

PRINTING YOUR DIARY ENTRIES

To print your diary entries, follow the instructions below:
1 Click on File and Print
2 In the Settings panel, select the option you want to use.
3 The panel on the right will change to reflect your choice.

VIDEO LINK

Check out the tutorial at www.brightredbooks.net/N5AdminIT for more.

ONLINE TEST

How well have you learned this topic? Take the test at www.brightredbooks.net/N5AdminIT

DON'T FORGET

Check out what your e-diary looks like in your own e-mail account – it might be different from the example shown.

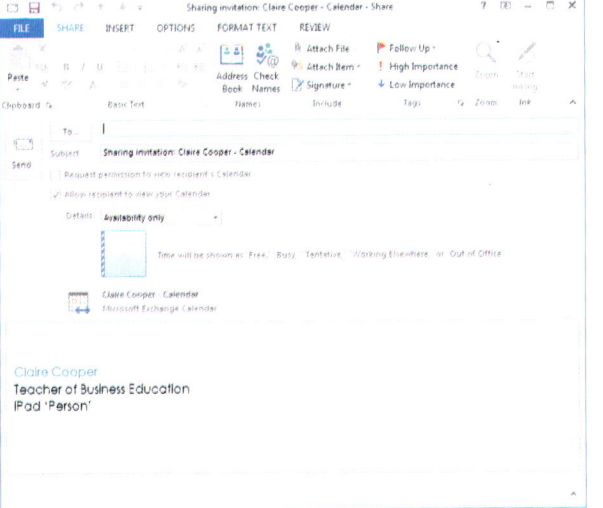

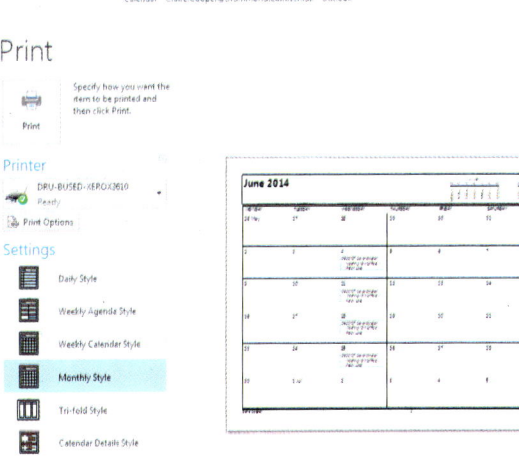

THINGS TO DO AND THINK ABOUT

Use your own e-diary or e-calendar to add in some events such as birthdays, celebrations and school dates for the year ahead.

KNOWLEDGE CHECK: USING ADVANCED FUNCTIONS OF TECHNOLOGY TO PREPARE AND COMMUNICATE INFORMATION

HOW DO I MEET THIS OUTCOME?

For Outcome 2 of this Unit, you are required to:

2   Use advanced functions of technology to prepare and communicate information to a professional standard by:

   2.1   Using functions of multimedia applications to create a presentation

   2.2   Using functions of desktop publishing to produce a document

   2.3   Using electronic methods to communicate information

Use the checklists and tasks below to evaluate your learning from this Outcome.

USING FUNCTIONS OF MULTIMEDIA APPLICATIONS TO CREATE A PRESENTATION: SKILL SCAN

		Green light	Amber light	Red light
2.1	I can insert, delete and edit text in presentation software.			
	I can format text.			
	I can insert and delete a graphic.			
	I can use bullets and numbers to enhance the presentation.			
	I can add and delete a slide and choose an appropriate slide layout.			
	I can apply slide transitions and animations.			
	I can import data from other packages.			
	I can change the slide content layout and the order of the slides.			
	I can apply a design scheme and background colour.			
	I can insert footer objects – Name, Slide Number, Date and Action Buttons.			

ONLINE

You can find presentation software activities in the Digital Zone at www.brightredbooks.net/N5AdminIT

USING FUNCTIONS OF DESKTOP PUBLISHING TO PRODUCE A DOCUMENT: SKILL SCAN

		Green light	Amber light	Red light
2.2	I can use desktop publishing software to produce a document, using the templates function.			
	I can set and change the margins in a document.			
	I can insert, delete, move and format text.			
	I can insert graphics.			
	I can insert headers and footers.			
	I can apply borders and shading to a document.			

ONLINE

You can find desktop publishing software activities at www.brightredbooks.net/N5AdminIT

ONLINE

You can find e-mail and e-diary activities at www.brightredbooks.net/N5AdminIT

USING ELECTRONIC METHODS TO COMMUNICATE INFORMATION: SKILL SCAN

		Green light	Amber light	Red light
2.3	I can access my e-mail account to compose and send a message.			
	I can access my address book to save e-mail addresses and to use this function to send e-mails.			
	I can use toolbar options to indicate the urgency of an e-mail.			
	I can add attachments to e-mails.			
	I can create a signature for my e-mails.			
	I can outline some example of emerging technologies – Blogs, Podcasts, Websites, Social Media and Virtual Learning Environments.			
	I can access my e-diary through my e-mail account and schedule an appointment.			
	I can set reminders for myself and schedule recurrent meetings.			
	I can access other users' calendars.			
	I can print extracts from my e-diary in daily, weekly and monthly view.			

THINGS TO DO AND THINK ABOUT

Be sure to make good use of this book and all of your course materials while you prepare for your National 5 assignment. You have all of the tools necessary to succeed and as long as you do your best you will achieve a grade of which you can be proud. Good luck!

COMMAND WORDS FOR NATIONAL 5 ADMINISTRATION AND IT

COMMAND WORDS ARE USED TO DIRECT YOU TO ANSWER QUESTIONS IN A PARTICULAR WAY.

Below we have provided a list of some of the Command Words which might be used and how you might present an answer.

Command word	In context of a question	Answer to question
List	List two principles of the Data Protection Act.	1. Data must be held securely. 2. Data must not be held for longer than is necessary.
Name	Name the type of training provided to all new employees.	Induction Training
Identify	Identify two security measures which can be taken to protect information in an organisation.	Authorised user ID's and passwords. Firewalls
State	State the purpose of a Visitors log.	The purpose of a visitors log is to record who is in the building for security and evacuation procedures.
Suggest	Suggest two consequences to an organisation of using unreliable information.	One consequence would be that the organisation could make poor decisions. A second consequence could be that the organisation's reputation could suffer.
Outline	Outline the purpose of sending out an Agenda before a meeting.	The purpose of an agenda is to inform those attending what will be discussed at the meeting allowing them to prepare fully.
Describe	Describe 2 advantages of using presentation software in a training session.	An advantage of using presentation software is that you can present text, graphics and video through this software. A second advantage is that you can printout copies of the slides for those who were unable to attend the training session.
Justify	Justify the use of an e-diary.	An e-diary is useful because you can set reminders for important events and the software will send a message or beep at an designated time – which a paper diary cannot do.
Compare	Compare a job description with a person specification.	A job description describes the key characteristics of the role itself, whereas, the person specification identifies the essential and desirable characteristics of the ideal candidate. Both these documents are used in the recruitment process.

a firewall is a network security system

establyshes a barrier between a trusted internal network a untrusted external work

GLOSSARY

absolute referencing

when you **don't** want spreadsheet software to automatically apply a formula to all the cells in each row or column, place dollar signs around the letter of the cell references you don't want changed.

address labels

used to send out several letters at the same time. Address labels are created by merging the information on a database of addresses into a word document and then printing this onto labels.

agenda

is attached to the notice of meeting and provides an outline of what will be discussed at the meeting.

anti-virus software

software that detects viruses, data loggers and other electronic dangers

blog

an online journal commonly used to record a person's thoughts and feelings on a particular topic or theme

browser

a software program installed on a device that allows you to access the internet

budget

an estimate of income and expenditure for a set period of time (used in the context of events in this guide)

business letter

a formal communication between an organisation and another interested party – for example, customers, shareholders, suppliers and employees. The template used for a business letter is called a letterhead.

business report

an internal business document that communicates the findings of an investigation or research project to those interested in the results

business terminology

business terms frequently used in N5 Administration and IT:

Term	Description
Quantity	This refers to the number of items held – sometimes used in the content of Stock or Sales.
	Quantity could be used in conjunction with Price to work out the Revenue or Total: = Quantity*Price
	Or it could be used to work out the total number of items held by the organisation: =QuantityJan+QuantityFeb+QuantityMar
Price	This refers to the value of an individual item – sometimes referred to as the Selling Price.
	Price is most commonly used in conjunction with a Quantity value to calculate Sales Revenue: = Price*Quantity
	It could also be used if calculating VAT: = Price * 20%

Term	Description
Revenue	Revenue is the term used to describe income generated from sales of goods and/or services by an organisation. It involves multiplying the quantity sold by the selling price.
Wages	This is the payment made to employees on a weekly, fortnightly or monthly basis. This is calculated by multiplying the number of hours worked by the rate of pay.
Salary	Some employees will be paid on the basis of an annual salary rather than on the basis of the hours they work. They normally have this annual amount paid in 12 equal instalments on a specific day or date of the month.
Income Tax	All UK citizens are required by law to pay Income Tax on their earnings through employment. This is deducted from the wages or salary payment and paid directly to UK Revenue and Customs. For accurate and up-to-date Income Tax bandings see: http://www.hmrc.gov.uk/rates/it.htm This is calculated as a percentage of Net Pay.
National Insurance	UK citizens pay a percentage of their earnings to cover National Insurance contributions, which entitle them to state benefits such as a state pension. To learn more about National Insurance visit: http://www.hmrc.gov.uk/ni/intro/basics.htm This is calculated as a percentage of Net Pay.
Net pay	This is the employee's wage or salary before any deductions. It is calculated either by dividing the Annual Salary amount by 12 or by multiplying the number of hours worked by the rate of pay.
Gross pay	This is the employee's wage or salary after deductions have been taken off. It is calculated by subtracting any deductions (such as Income Tax and National Insurance) from the Net Pay.
Bonus	This is an amount of money paid to an employee if they have met certain pre-defined criteria. A bonus is paid in addition to their wage or salary. It is normally calculated as a percentage of annual salary or earnings.
Commission	This is an amount of money paid to an employee if they have met sales targets. Commission is paid in addition to any wage/salary or bonus. It is normally calculated as a percentage of the overall Sales figures.
Discount	A discount is a deduction from another value. A Sales discount is when an organisation reduces the selling price to encourage more customers to buy.
Valued Added Tax (VAT)	This is a tax on most UK good and services. The current standard rate of VAT is 20%. To learn more about VAT visit· http://www.hmrc.gov.uk/vat/start/introduction.htm

contd

Term	Description
Rate of pay **Hourly rate** **Piece rate**	These three terms all refer to the rate of pay an employee receives, depending on their employee contract. Rate of pay and hourly rate tend to refer to the amount a person is paid per hour of work, and in some cases this would be the National Minimum Wage. For an up-to-date figure for this visit: https://www.gov.uk/national-minimum-wage-rates Piece rate refers to the amount paid to an employee per finished item they have sold or produced.
Pension contributions	Pension contributions are classed as a deduction from earnings to contribute to pension payments made to the employee on retirement. These are normally calculated as a percentage of earnings/salary and will vary depending on the pension scheme that the employee is part of.

cell reference
sometimes referred to as a cell address, a cell reference consists of the column letter and row number where the cell is located

certificates
used to acknowledge an individual's participation in an event or to acknowledge their performance in an assessment

charting
the graphic representation of numerical data. Charts can be used to present data in a format that is easy to read and interpret, and can also be used to highlight trends in the data. Spreadsheets enable you to create a variety of charts from their data.

collate
collect and combine (usually information)

comprehensive
including or dealing with all or nearly all elements or aspects of something

Computer Misuse Act 1990
This Act prohibits unlawful access to computer systems. It is illegal to:
- gain access to computer systems without permission
- gain access to computer systems with the intention of committing a criminal offence
- gain access to computer systems to change or alter details without permission
- make, provide and supply any materials or equipment that could be used to facilitate a computer misuse offence.

consequence
a result or effect of something

curriculum vitae (CV)
a document prepared by an individual who is looking for employment. This document will detail the person's skills, qualities, experience and qualifications.

customer service
the process of ensuring that the customer feels that the product or service they have bought has met or exceeded their expectations. Customer service is the process of ensuring that the customer feels that the product or service they have bought has met or exceeded their expectations.

Data Protection Act 1998
This Act states that organisations which hold personal data must ensure that the data is:
- held fairly and lawfully
- only used for the purpose registered with the Information Commissioner
- adequate, relevant and not excessive
- accurate
- not held for longer than is necessary
- held securely
- processed in line with the data subjects rights
- not transferred outside the EEA (European Economic Area).

database
software designed to store large amounts of data electronically so that it can be accessed by different users and presented in different ways

datasheet view
the view in spreadsheet software that enables you to see all the records

demotivated
when somebody becomes less eager to work or study

design view
the view in spreadsheet software that enables you to see the Field Names and Data Types

desktop publishing (DTP)
software used to place and manipulate text and graphics on your computer to produce print-ready, high-quality materials.

diversity
a range of different things

e-diary
an electronic scheduling tool that is normally linked to your e-mail account. It helps you to keep track of important dates, times of meetings and tasks with deadlines. Everyone in a team can share their e-diaries.

e-mail
The Oxford Online Dictionary defines e-mail as: 'Messages distributed by electronic means from one computer user to one or more recipients via a network.'

emphasis animation
in a presentation, this animates the text or object of a particular slide to emphasise it.

encryption
used to transfer sensitive data across the internet

entrance animation
in a presentation, this animates the text or object as it appears on screen.

evaluation form
a way of gathering factual, quantitative data that often uses 'closed' questions

event
in the context of Administration and IT, an event is a planned assembly of people, brought together for a related purpose or cause

event planning
has three key steps:
1 Planning – all tasks carried out **before** the event
2 Supporting – all tasks carried **during** the event
3 Follow up – all tasks carried out **after** the event

exit animation
in a presentation, this animates the text/objects before you move onto the next slide

favourites and bookmarks
are browser functions that allow you to save a link to a web page that you access regularly, or would like to access again in the future.

feedback form
a way of gathering informal, qualitative data that often uses 'open-ended' questions.

firewalls
ensure that hackers cannot access the company computers

foreign key
a field in a spreadsheet that is used to link tables together when creating relationships

form
a document that is designed to collect information from another person or group of people. It can be designed to be completed by hand or electronically. There are many different forms used in business:
- Application form
- Accident Report form
- Travel and accommodation booking form
- Expenses claim form

function
a pre-set formula in spreadsheet software. Functions include:
- SUM
- AVERAGE
- MAX
- MIN
- COUNT (NUMBERS)

Health and Safety at Work Act (HASAWA) 1974
businesses are legally bound by the Health and Safety at Work Act (HASAWA) 1974. This legislation is in place to ensure that employers provide a safe working environment for their employees to work in.

house style
a standard layout that an organisation uses in all of its documentation to ensure that everything it sends out to customers looks consistent, professional and instantly recognisable.

hyperlinks
used to move quickly between different pages on a website or around the internet in general.

IF statements
help to test a condition that is specified in a spreadsheet to see if it's true or false. If the condition is true, the function will carry out one action. If the condition is false, it will carry out a different action. You can then make a decision based on this information.

induction training
new recruits to a company need basic induction training so that they know how to work safely. This includes finding out about arrangements for first aid, fire and evacuation.

inventory
a complete list of items such as property, goods in stock, or the contents of a building

itinerary
a travel document that details the journey the person is taking, step by step.

job description
outlines the background to the role, the tasks/duties to be carried out, the employee's responsibilities and who they report to. It might also include their days/hours of work, pay grade and benefits.

line spacing
is the amount of space between each line. You can select the amount of line spacing you require – for example:
- 1   (single space)
- 1.5   (one-and-a-half space)
- 2   (double space)

manuscript corrections
a standard set of correction marks to show what editing is required:

Symbol/ sign	Meaning	Action
the	Delete	Do not type any words that have a line through them.
⟨ a	Insert	Insert the word/s written beside the symbol - ⟨
⟨ #	Insert space	Insert a space in the text indicated by the symbol.
⌒	Close up	Delete space/s in the text.
NP [	New paragraph	Start a new paragraph, where indicated in the text.
⌢	Run on	Join the paragraphs together.
trs	Transpose	Move the letter/s or word/s as indicated with the underlines.
Stet	Let it stand	Type the word/s with the broken line underneath – ignore the other alterations.
UC or CAPS	Upper case	Change the letter/s or word/s indicated in the text to capital letters.
LC	Lower case	Change the letter/s indicated in the text to small letters.
Bold/ italics/ underline		Where this is indicated in the margin, an area of the text will be underlined – only format the underlined section.

GLOSSARY

memorandum

a word-processed document that is used to communicate information internally between different departments or between management and staff

minute of a meeting

a written account of what was discussed at a meeting

mystery shopper

a person who is hired to visit a shop in disguise to assess the quality of the goods or services.

name badges

created in a similar way to address labels for people attending a conference or training event, for example.

non-printing guidelines

a feature of dtp software - you can use them to align text and graphics boxes on screen, but they don't appear when you print the document.

notice of a meeting

sent out to those attending a meeting to inform them of the purpose of the meeting and when and where it will be held

person specification

details the skills, qualities, qualifications and experience that a suitable candidate is required to have

podcast

an audio recording that can be downloaded to your phone or mobile device, so you can listen to it when it's convenient for you

primary key

a field in a spreadsheet containing information that is unique to the record it is attached to. Examples include Customer Reference Numbers, National Insurance Numbers and SQA Numbers.

priorities list

a list of required tasks that are prioritised by importance or by deadlines.

quality

a personal characteristic – an aspect of your personality

relationship

a way of linking information between two tables

relative referencing

this applies a formula or formulae to all the cells in each row or column

repetitive strain injury

a term used to describe pain in the muscles, tendons and nerves. It is often caused by tasks of a repetitive nature such as using a keyboard, by poor posture or by incorrect positioning of seating.

retain

to keep hold of something

search engine

helps you to find what you need by searching all the web pages available against criteria you have entered, and by filtering the results for you.

skill

an ability that is gained through learning and training

slide transition

the process of moving between two slides in a presentation. Different types of slide transition can give your presentation a more controlled feel, and can also improve the experience for the viewer.

social media

essentially designed to allow people to share their lives with friends, family and business colleagues online – and to make new friends or contacts. Some examples of these are Facebook, Twitter, Instagram and Linkedin.

spreadsheet

an electronic document in which data is arranged in the rows and columns of a grid and can be manipulated and used in calculations. This software allows the user to perform complex calculations through the use of formulae and functions. Spreadsheets can be used to prepare financial statements and budgets.

You can also use spreadsheet software to create visual aids such as charts and graphs.

template

a document that has been prepared in advance, and that often contains key information about a business.

text alignment

how text is lined up. Text is normally aligned to the left but you can highlight blocks of text and highlight them to the right, centre or on both sides.

to-do lists

a list of the tasks that have to be completed in a project

venue

place where an organised event is held

virtual learning environments (VLEs)

require the user to login to a secure area to access resources and tools to support their learning. iTunesU, Edmodo and GLOW are all VLEs.

vodcast

a video recording that can be downloaded so you can view it when it's convenient for you.

website

a dedicated site on a specific topic or theme. Websites have specific addresses on the internet called URLs – uniform resource locators.

wildcard

a special character used in a spreadsheet query that can stand for either a single character or a string of text.

workbook

a spreadsheet file.

worksheet

a single page within a spreadsheet file.